The Vietnamese and Their Revolution

The Vietnamese

Written Under the Auspices
of the Center of International Studies,
Princeton University

and Their Revolution

by John T. McAlister, Jr.
and Paul Mus

Harper Torchbooks ❧
Harper & Row, Publishers
New York, Evanston, and London

THE VIETNAMESE AND THEIR REVOLUTION. Copyright © 1970 by John T. McAlister, Jr. and the estate of Paul Mus. All rights reserved. Printed in the United States of America. No part of this book may be used or reproduced in any manner whatsoever without written permission except in the case of brief quotations embodied in critical articles and reviews. For information address Harper & Row, Publishers, Inc., 49 East 33rd Street, New York, N.Y. 10016. Published simultaneously in Canada by Fitzhenry & Whiteside Limited, Toronto.

First Edition: HARPER TORCHBOOKS, 1970,
Harper & Row, Publishers, Inc.,
New York, N.Y. 10016.

LIBRARY OF CONGRESS CATALOG CARD NUMBER: 74–103920

CONTENTS

To the Memory of Our Fathers

CYPRIEN MUS
(1872–1939)

The First Man to Welcome Captain Dreyfus
Home to the Vaucluse from Devil's Island

J. T. McALISTER
(1894–1966)

Who Lies in the South Carolina Soil
He Loved and Made Abundant

FOREWORD

When I reached the top of the stairs, I could see at a distance down the dimly lit corridor his shadowy figure blocking off the late afternoon sun as it streamed through a nearby window. He was motionless as though in a trance. As I got closer I could tell that he was standing with the tips of his shoes pressed into the wall and his face nearly buried in a bulletin board. I had heard that he practiced yoga, but not, I thought, in the corridor of the Hall of Graduate Studies—at least not on a sunny autumn afternoon.

My approach startled him, and in a flash he wheeled around exchanging the pair of eyeglasses he wore for another he held in his hand. At a glance both pairs looked so thick that they seemed like the bottom of soda-pop bottles stuck into frames.

"Professor Mus?" I asked in a hesitant voice. As he responded gently, I wondered about him. His eyesight was so poor that he could not even read a bulletin board without pressing his face into it. Was this the man I had been told about? The man who had parachuted behind Japanese lines in Viet Nam to organize a resistance to the wartime occupation? The man who had sought out Ho Chi Minh in the rugged mountains of northern Viet Nam to negotiate with him to prevent a war in the country? It couldn't be.

"I'd like to take your course on Viet Nam," I stammered in disbelief that I had found Paul Mus. The year was 1957, and I was a college senior at Yale. Almost nobody in America knew much about Viet Nam, and I was no exception. But I had learned enough to know that Mus, a French professor who annually spent one semester in New Haven, was probably the most knowledgeable scholar in the world on Viet Nam and that his courses at Yale were generally neglected except for a small handful of graduate students.

The moment I met him I was immediately struck by the strong

sense of paradox that was Paul Mus's most conspicuous characteristic. His appearance was a startling contradiction to the active,
indeed dangerous, life he had led. Besides miserably poor eyesight,
he was awkward and uncoordinated. His bulky frame moved in
jerky motions which suggested that he was totally alien to a world
of action and physical toughness. His flat, round, open face was
too kindly and sympathetic to be that of a man who had matched
wits with Ho Chi Minh, Japanese occupation forces, and Communist-
led guerrillas.

The paradox between Mus's appearance and his active life was,
however, a perfect introduction to him. It conveyed the essence of
his personality and gave the key to the way he approached his profession of scholar and teacher. People are so fascinated by paradox,
he had found, that it was easier to communicate with them by
arousing their curiosity through seemingly incredible statements.
Besides, it was more fun. Paradox offered the opportunity for
humor, which Mus used in a whimsical and teasing way to simplify
complex issues. Since the cultural basis of contemporary conflict
in Viet Nam and adjacent Southeast Asian countries contains complexities beyond the interest of most people, Mus's style gave these
issues a liveliness which they otherwise would not have had.

There was great excitement in becoming one of Paul Mus's handful of students. He filled his lectures and classroom discussions with
absorbing stories that turned the dry facts of such things as Vietnamese village life into vivid portraits of believable people. No longer
were the Vietnamese remote and unpredictable. Their seemingly
chaotic life came more clearly into focus through Mus's careful
explanation of why the values which once held them together had
declined in vitality without there being any new values to take their
place. Against this background the paradoxical qualities of the
Vietnamese seemed merely superficial aspects of a profound human
predicament—one which people groping toward new values for
modern lives throughout the world shared. Mus's greatness as a
teacher and scholar was his capacity to portray this predicament in
compelling human terms through both analytical insights and fascinating stories of his personal experiences.

Like any other "true believer" I was anxious that others know about Mus. Yet he never became widely known, because all but a few of his writings on Viet Nam were in French. This was a part of the Mus paradox that was confounding and frustrating. In the late 1950's, before Viet Nam became America's most pressing issue of national concern, Mus's knowledge was primarily a matter of academic interest. But as the United States became more deeply involved in Viet Nam I felt an increasing anguish that Mus's insights into Vietnamese character and society were not available to an audience of American readers. My anguish was heightened even further by the mixed quality of the spate of books on Viet Nam that did appear and which did become part of the public debate over the war.

Despite nearly two decades of teaching in the United States, Mus never felt compelled either to translate his important writings into English or to write a book about Viet Nam especially for an American audience. He always turned aside suggestions of his writing for Americans with the comment that his research on the early civilizations of Southeast Asia would be of more enduring scholarly significance, or that a Frenchman had no right to involve himself in American politics. Naturally, I never found any of these explanations very satisfactory. So, finally, I persuaded him to give me permission to sponsor a translation of his most important work on the Vietnamese, *Viet Nam: sociologie d'une guerre,* published in 1952 during a critical phase of the French-Indochina war.

This book is the most thorough analysis of the cultural foundations of Vietnamese politics that ever has been or probably ever will be written. In it Mus demonstrated a depth of knowledge and experience that no one else has matched. But he also wrote the book in such a complicated style that even those Americans fluent in French —and Frenchmen too—have had a difficult time absorbing its full meaning. I was convinced that these stylistic problems could be overcome through a careful translation which would clarify obscure points and infuse some of the liveliness of Mus's classroom discussion into the presentation. Aware of my own inadequacies as a translator I decided to call upon a top-ranked professional, Mme. June Guicharnaud, who has translated most of the writings of André Gide into English. By assisting her with substantive points, I felt that the project could be completed with few difficulties and with great benefit to the growing American preoccupation with Viet Nam.

When, after several weeks of intense but unsatisfying effort, Mme. Guicharnaud concluded that the book was too complex to be translated, I was dejected. "Mus's style is more complicated than Proust's," she said. Although she wanted me to find some other translator, I knew this would be a fruitless task. Mme. Guicharnaud, the wife of a distinguished professor of French at Yale, had been charmed by Mus and had accepted the challenge of the translation with enthusiasm and dedication. I felt certain there was no one more competent or committed than she. So, I pleaded with her to go on or at least to work out some way of bringing Mus's insights about Vietnamese society to the attention of American readers.

The arrangement we reached has resulted in this book. Without Mme. Guicharnaud's patient and diligent effort this book would never have been possible, and the wisdom of Paul Mus would never have been available to Americans. Instead of a translation, the focus of attention was narrowed to a thorough rewriting of what I considered the most vital portions of *Viet Nam: sociologie d'une guerre,* which amounted to about one-third of the whole. Mme. Guicharnaud agreed to make a rough, literal translation of these chapters, which I then completely reorganized and rewrote. Ideas and information were relocated, some chapters were literally torn apart and their contents reconstituted in a new framework, other chapters were expanded so extensively that they lost all but a trace of their original form. The guiding purpose was to capture the essence of Mus's thought and present it in as simple and forceful a style as possible. The result was an entirely new book.

Only after the manuscript was complete did Mus see how I had presented what I considered the essence of his knowledge on Viet Nam. Although he approved and urged publication, I bear sole responsibility for the shortcomings of what appears here. If this book is as valuable as I think it is, then it is due to Mus's wisdom as a scholar and his sensitivity as a teacher. In writing it, I have tried to act as his interpreter, drawing upon my understanding of his knowledge as well as my own scholarship on Viet Nam.

I have made all of the judgments about organization and have

written all of the contents, including substantial rewriting of two
articles from scholarly journals which Mus originally published in
English and which I felt should be part of the book. The Prologue
and Epilogue, which attempt to provide a context for Mus's thought,
are entirely my own. Because of my role in preparing the book, Mus
insisted that my name appear as principal coauthor, though I would
have preferred that his name appear alone. In every sense this is his
book, because without him I probably would never have become a
scholar on Viet Nam.

The preparation of the book has been sponsored by the Center of
International Studies, Princeton University; I wish to express my
gratefulness to the Center's former director, Professor Klaus Knorr,
and to Professor Harry Eckstein, for their support of the project.
The Center not only provided the funds to support my work on the
book but also that of Mme. Guicharnaud. In the final stages of
writing, I was supported in part by a grant from the Joint Committee
on Asian Studies of the American Council of Learned Societies-
Social Science Research Council, which it is a great pleasure to
acknowledge here.

For permission to use portions of *Viet Nam: sociologie d'une
guerre* in a reorganized and rewritten form, I wish to thank the
book's publisher, Editions du Seuil of Paris. For permission to include two of Mus's articles in substantially revised form I wish to
thank the editors of *Pacific Affairs* and the *Yale Review*. Two close
friends, Professor Frederick W. Mote of Princeton University and
Mr. William A. K. Lake of Washington, D.C., offered many helpful
comments on an early version of the manuscript for which I am most
appreciative. John Jay Iselin and Hugh Van Dusen of Harper and
Row provided welcome encouragement, splendid editorial advice,
and the rapid transformation of a messy manuscript into an attrac-
tive book. Finally, I cannot acknowledge too often or too strongly
my special gratitude to Mme. June Guicharnaud for her decisive
contribution in the making of the book.

The thrill of completing this book and adding a fresh perspective
to Viet Nam for American readers has been overshadowed by a
heavy sadness. As the book was going to press, Paul Mus suffered
another in a series of heart attacks and, at a provincial hospital in

Avignon on August 9, he died. Despite the turbulence of his times and some personal misfortune, he lived an enviable life filled with adventure, reflection, and satisfaction at having encompassed more than his share of human experience. For those in whose hearts Paul Mus's spirit will remain a living presence, the publication in English of a summation of his knowledge on Viet Nam may serve to remind us of the vitality of a man who touched us deeply. I only regret that, in addition to her grief, Mme. Suzanne Mus had to bear the burden of making some final arrangements for publication.

JOHN T. McALISTER, JR.

Center of International Studies
Woodrow Wilson School of Public and International Affairs
Princeton University
October 15, 1969

The Vietnamese and Their Revolution

Prologue:

Politics and Revolution in Viet Nam

Revolution in Viet Nam has seen an unending repetition of some now familiar patterns of politics. Events and people have changed but the patterns have remained virtually the same. These patterns are the modern form taken by an age-old factional struggle for power among the Vietnamese—not just for power itself but for the way power will be held and shared. Though foreign powers have tried to separate the factions into different regions, this division has been largely artificial, because the essence of the struggle is not so much between regions as it is between segments of society. Since power has been so diffuse and difficult to organize by any of these factions, the struggle has already endured for a quarter of a century and is unlikely to be resolved soon. Underlying this struggle and producing its repetition of familiar political patterns are values common to all Vietnamese. Despite the turbulence of twenty-five years of revolution these common values have persisted, although they have not gone unchallenged. Indeed, the competition to change the values by which the Vietnamese live is what the revolution is all about.

As resilient as they are, Viet Nam's traditional values have been inadequate to organize the power to sustain a modern government unifying all Vietnamese within one nation. Unity by itself, of course, carries no certainty that there will be an end to factional struggles for power. But without unity, factional struggles will surely persist, because there is virtually no means for successfully isolating the contending parties from one another. Unity, moreover, is the goal of both major factions in the struggle, since each side is trying to prevail over the other, not just in a region but throughout the whole country. Both sides realize implicitly that unity depends on the creation of a modern state which can satisfy enough demands of the Vietnamese people to win everyone's allegiance. Therefore, in fighting for the most certain possible means for holding power, the two principal competitors in the revolutionary struggle in Viet Nam have both been seeking the same goal: the creation of a modern state out of a tradition-bound society. Because a modern state will depend on a new feeling of community among the Vietnamese, the winner of the struggle will surely be the side that can transform the vestigial remains of a long-decayed communal spirit into a new sense of Viet Nam as a nation.

New communities require new values to link people together in a bond of common purpose. In Viet Nam, a confirmation of new values is being sought by two competitor governments, one in Hanoi, the other in Saigon, each of which hopes to become *the* modern leader for all Viet Nam. Their search is not an act of contemplation but a struggle to win commitment through political rewards proportional to performance in organizing power on the basis of new values. The struggle is far from over; human values rarely change quickly, and the experience of Viet Nam is no exception. But though this revolutionary struggle has frequently seemed like unintelligible chaos, there have been recurrent patterns of action which result from the very traditions that each side must try to transform if they are to create the framework for a new sense of community.

This book is an effort to identify and explain recurrent patterns in Viet Nam's revolution through a study of the problems of creating such a new community out of the vestiges of a persisting tradition of politics. The book is the product of two minds, one French and the other American. It is the result of two separate experiences in Viet Nam, decades apart in time but intimately interwoven through the common perspective of a French teacher and his American student. Times change, people and events are no longer what they once were. Yet in the characteristics that are fundamental to Vietnamese life there have been very few basic changes. Revolution in Viet Nam has, in fact, been prolonged, intense, and brutal because change has been so hard to achieve. Whether one is out of date in his views of Viet Nam, therefore, is a question of what aspect of Vietnamese life one is looking at. Warlords have come and gone, prime ministers have faded from the scene, new hopes have been aroused, old "approaches" discarded, and fresh starts initiated. The colonially minded French have left and the vigorous-minded Americans have come.

But in the relationship between the three-fourths of the Vietnamese who live in bamboo-encircled villages scattered throughout the rich green-brown deltas and the governments encased in the tree-shaded, yellow stucco cities there have been few changes. This basic dichotomy between the life of the cities—outposts of modernity in an alien world of archaic tradition—and the life of the village is the focus of attention of this book. Across the gap of time, space, and culture separating the countryside from the cities, pro-Western urban governments have tried to project their strength through programs of political control and counter-guerrilla military operations. Despite the determined efforts of a quarter of a century none of these programs has been successful, nor have these discredited techniques even been changed very much in their essential characteristics from one era to another. Just like the French in the late 1940's, the Americans in the late 1960's boasted unjustifiably of the results of "pacification" programs designed to bring the countryside under government control.

This struggle by pro-Western, urban-oriented governments to gain control over the countryside from village-based revolutionaries has been the most basic recurrent pattern of the twenty-five years of warfare in Viet Nam. The struggle has persisted because few rural people have felt any real stake in the activities of the urban governments. Yet at the outset of revolution in 1945 almost all rural people were uncommitted to any faction. They lived lives limited by the social horizons of their native village as well as by the routine of growing rice in the irrigated fields nearby. Their lack of commitment was not, however, a congenial mode of life; Vietnamese seem instinctively to feel the need to be a part of a larger cultural community than the village. Perhaps this longing is due to the loneliness of rural life or its uncertainty, but whatever the source, the result is that Vietnamese consider the creation of new communities not as political acts but as spiritual ones. The explanation, therefore, of why a peasant people with a deep sense of spirituality would become committed to mass participation in a national movement that was more overtly political than any in their previous history is the story of revolution in Viet Nam. It is also the reason for this book.

The chapters that form the central portions of this book were originally written in French in 1952 by Paul Mus, who had, at the time, recently stepped down as the political adviser to the French high command in Viet Nam. Mus's departure from that colonially inclined French establishment, a group that still referred to Viet Nam by its colonial name of Indochina, was neither harmonious nor unexpected. His advice was not accepted; in fact it had virtually never been accepted on any of the really critical issues of French policy. But Mus knew more about the Vietnamese than any other Frenchman, and it was nice to know that he was around even if his judgments failed to confirm the wisdom of policies which France was determined to follow. Increasingly, however, Mus became a nuisance to his superiors. They had little patience with his unflagging insistence that French policies were based on completely wrong assumptions about Vietnamese society. They had a job to do: save as much French influence over the Vietnamese as they could. Mus didn't understand, they said; he wasn't on the team. With characteristic perceptiveness, he resigned before they had a chance to fire him.

The resignation of a political adviser in Viet Nam whose advice is not being accepted hardly sounds like an unusual event. For decades all sorts of forlorn former officials have been claiming that if only their advice had been followed the war could have been won and all the subsequent agony could have been avoided. Does anyone take these voices from the past very seriously? What makes Paul Mus any different from the others? And even if he is distinctive in his views, why should anyone be concerned almost twenty years later about what Mus had to say on the follies of French policy in Viet Nam? Isn't it obvious to everyone that

France failed in Viet Nam because it sought colonial domination and, in the process, gave the Communists such a foothold that subsequent pro-Western regimes, weakened by a persisting French mentality of laxity on corruption and military preparedness, could not be saved despite truly massive American support? Is there anything more that can be said about Viet Nam that hasn't already been said?

Yes, there is. What has been repeatedly said about Viet Nam has been written almost exclusively from a very particular Western perspective—a perspective that has as its most distinctive feature a fetish about time. There is a sense of urgency in these Western reports over the mere passage of time itself and a feeling that events occurring within a certain span of time must have at least the same importance as events that occur within a similar period in Western countries. Of course, this urgency has been heightened even further by war and by the understandable human desire to see war stopped. Americans, in particular, have not experienced until Viet Nam—at least not since the American Revolution—a war that has lasted longer than four years. American expectations about time, therefore, have governed much of the writing about Viet Nam and have especially caused writers to focus on those aspects of war and politics which have been changing the fastest. Yet the speed with which change has occurred has been no real indication of the importance of change. Those things changing the fastest have most often been examples of futile and misdirected efforts to achieve fundamental, and therefore significant, changes. Futility has resulted simply because of an urgency to get positive results in a short amount of time. As a result, readers have become frustrated and uninterested by those predictable reports that dwell on the hopelessness of change as judged by Western standards.

Americans have not, of course, been unaware of Vietnamese antipathies toward the Western sense of urgency or concept of time. Many an American officer in Viet Nam has displayed conspicuously on his desk the quotation from Kipling which promises frustration to the man who tries to hurry the East. Despite such whimsical concessions, however, Americans have rarely doubted that the Vietnamese *should* adopt our sense of urgency and in fact *would* do so if only we were determined and forceful enough to persuade them that we would stand for nothing less. Yet precisely because there has been little understanding of what in fact does motivate the Vietnamese and give them a sense of urgency, American determination has resulted in frustration and failure in Viet Nam.

Nearly everyone agrees that the Vietnamese are energetic and tenacious workers when they are motivated, a situation which is hardly infrequent, especially for the peasants in their fields. And a continuing theme of American military leaders has been that the war in Viet Nam is a political contest to win the spirit of the Vietnamese people—or, as they put it in cliché form, "to win the hearts and minds of the people." But virtually every American effort over the past decade has betrayed a fundamental ignorance of what does animate the hearts and minds of the Vietnamese people and how their spirit can be won.

The spirit or mentality of the Vietnamese—the three-fourths of them who continue to lead lives rooted in the traditions of the village—is the essential untold story about Viet Nam. The reason for telling this story is not to rekindle the fight for the countryside or to lay the basis for any particular set of policy recommendations—it is to emphasize that the participation of peasants in a revolution to create a modern state is the story of most of Asia in this century. No one thought that the march of peasants into modern lives would be a peaceful event, but few realized that this transformation of a rural people's role in their society would become confused with Communism—or rather with a view of Communism as an international conspiracy orchestrated from world centers. Now that the United States has learned the hard way that massive force can at best achieve only a stalemate against a peasant-based revolution, the original problem of bringing peasants into a modern society remains to be resolved—now through political accommodation rather than military confrontation. If this task is to be fulfilled with a minimum of violence, attention must be focused on those aspects of Vietnamese life that can explain the most about the changes villagers are seeking as well as the kind of motivation and sense of urgency that is propelling them.

It should come as no surprise that the most perceptive insights into these traditions which Vietnamese villagers have drawn upon most heavily in their transitional path to revolution were written nearly twenty years ago in French by Paul Mus. After all that has happened in Viet Nam, Americans have come to expect the ironic as being almost typical of the way things occur there. And though there is indeed great irony in the fact that Mus's perceptive writings have been overlooked in the rush to dream up American policy panaceas, there is nothing ironic about the uniqueness of his insights. Mus has had an opportunity to understand the Vietnamese and come to grips with their character which is unmatched by any other Westerner, especially Americans, who have as a nation only recently become interested in Viet Nam. His experience with the Vietnamese goes back to the first decade of this century, when he came with his parents to the colony of Indochina as a small child. His own growth to maturity paralleled the rise of Vietnamese nationalist and revolutionary movements, particularly the one led by Ho Chi Minh—twelve years Mus's senior and with whom Mus would have a critically important rendezvous in an effort to prevent the outbreak of the war that continues today.

Paul Mus's father had been sent by the French government to Viet Nam at a time when "divide and rule" was the hallmark of colonial policy. France had severed Viet Nam into three parts, called Tonkin, Annam, and Cochin China, immersed into a French-run colonial territory known as Indochina, which also included Cambodia and Laos. Any Vietnamese who uttered the real name of his country was subject to suspicion or arrest; the French referred to the people they ruled by the perjorative term "Annamese." "Viet Nam" was, therefore, a clandestine word and a rallying cry for revolutionaries who wanted desperately to overthrow French control and modernize the country.

In these twilight years just before the August guns of World War I ended an era, France was feeling the full vigor of its civilizing mission in the tropical world. Intent on putting its cultural stamp on Viet Nam, France decided to create a Western education system to train Vietnamese in French traditions and technical knowledge. The elder Mus was selected for the seminal post of establishing the system, and in 1907 he opened the first high school in Viet Nam, from which, over a decade later, his son Paul would graduate along with his Vietnamese childhood friends. Such was the confidence in education in that era that the elder Mus could not have realized his freshly built schools would become the breeding ground for a new generation of revolutionary nationalists as well as the Francophile upper-class Vietnamese, who would later selfishly side with France against their revolutionary brethren. The first inkling of what the future held came in 1931, when the French-educated founder of Viet Nam's first nationalist political party, Nguyen Thai Hoc, went to his death beneath a French guillotine screaming, "Viet Nam! Viet Nam!"

These first signs of revolutionary upheaval were still more than a decade ahead when Paul Mus graduated from high school in Hanoi in 1919. No Frenchmen, at least none who recorded his views at the time, anticipated the convulsion that lay before them as the twentieth century unfolded in Viet Nam. The seventeen-year-old Mus was no exception. As he made his plans for the future, the political destiny of Viet Nam—revolutionary or otherwise—never crossed his mind. Politics, of course, as a vocation for a Frenchman in Viet Nam was a hopeless prospect for a young man planning his life's career. And for Mus, Viet Nam, the land of his childhood, was the only land he knew and the only place he expected to live. Any career he chose would be a career he could follow in Viet Nam. Mus was French by birth, citizenship, and language, but he knew France only through the stories of his parents and their friends. His textbooks told him the history of a faraway land, a land that was somehow his own and that he would fruitlessly, yet courageously, defend as a young officer on the Belgian frontier in 1940. But France was not as real or compelling to him as the land of unending rice fields dotted here and there with villages and broken only by mountains, sea, and infrequent cities to which he had come at the age of five and spent his formative years.

In an odyssey that would often lead him away from this village world and would finally exile him forever from Viet Nam, Mus began a career that became a tireless quest for understanding the land of his childhood. Why such a quest? Perhaps Mus expected to find some lost thread of his youthful experience. Perhaps, like every man, he hoped to capture a childhood dream and make it his own. Or perhaps the rhythm of the peasant world held a secret whose answer he felt he must find—a secret that peasants, despite the deceptive simplicity of their lives, seem to hide behind their bashful smiles. A secret which had produced the most astonishing architectural achievements in the world in those exquisitely detailed and delicately constructed monuments like Angkor Wat in Cambodia, Barabudur in Java, and lesser ones in Viet Nam. Here are monuments of such magnificent beauty that their grandeur stands forth in incomprehensible contrast to the humble lives of the peasants in the surrounding villages. What secret can explain such a contrast?

In seeking answers many Westerners have shared the frustration of that first Frenchman who a hundred years ago stumbled across the ruins of Angkor Wat deep in the Cambodian jungle. When he demanded in stunned bewilderment how the hundreds of acres of breathtakingly beautiful monuments had gotten there, he received a startling reply. "They just grew there," a sardonic peasant teasingly responded. What power, what knowledge did such frail people have which they hinted at humorously but never revealed? How could they once have had the capacity to build such eloquent monuments and yet never tried to soften the austerity of their lives? What continues to give them such a sense of cohesiveness and confidence and what is the source of their strength to sustain the rigorous routine of one harvest after another? If Paul Mus was to come to terms with the land of his childhood, he would have to come to terms with the lives of peasants who, half a century after he began his career, as in the long centuries before, still are three-fourths of the country's population.

Paradox, like that in the contrast between the seeming simplicity of the peasants of Southeast Asia and the artistic creations of their past, became the leading hallmark of the quest Mus set for himself. Paradox, moreover, has been the natural link to those he has wanted to reach with his knowledge of Southeast Asia. Most people, because they find fascination in the apparent mystery of paradoxical situations, delight in tales which play upon seemingly unexplained contradictions of human experience. Throughout his life, Paul Mus skillfully emphasized in his own subtle and charming way the paradoxical aspects of Southeast Asian life. But he indulged his readers and listeners in these playful attributes of his storytelling with a distinct purpose in mind: to rid them, painlessly, of their innocent preconceptions about a land that has now violently intruded itself into distant consciences. Yet, at the very beginning, Mus himself had to learn to distinguish between myth and preconception and true essence; he had to sort out the misconceptions of his childhood and test them against the knowledge of the times. And doing so involved a minor paradox of its own. To study the culture of Southeast Asia meant that he would have to leave the land of his childhood and set out for a capital he had never known.

When Mus arrived in Paris for the first time in the summer of 1919, a stranger to the city that was and is the heart and mind and soul of France, he was a seventeen-year-old student in search of a university education. So intent on his mission was he that he hardly realized the city was preoccupied with the work of the plenipotentiaries at Versailles who thought they were organizing a peace that would end war. Of course, Mus was concerned about the future of Europe, but since he had not endured the war and since he planned to return to Southeast Asia, he could hardly be blamed for being more concerned about his studies.

Archaeology, religion, philosophy, and Asian languages were the four corners of his intellectual foundation; mastery over them would transform his boyish dreams into a manly career as a scholar and savant of Southeast Asian culture. Through archaeology he would acquire the competence to confront the decaying ruins of those awesome architectural monuments at Angkor and elsewhere and extract their hidden secrets. Religion and philosophy would provide the sensitivity to assess the secrets which these monuments held and to relate these rhythmic architectural forms to the vitality of the life of the people that lived about them. Asian languages—

Sanskrit and Chinese especially—were also essential tools if the inscriptions which adorned the monuments were to be unraveled and their messages added to a young scholar's growing fund of knowledge.

Despite the seriousness of his quest for an intellectual knowledge of Southeast Asian culture, Mus was not indifferent to the charms of Paris and he did not turn his back on his French heritage while there. He also did not become a bookish, humorless person; indeed his whole effort was an extension of a lively personality that sought the fulfillment of a long-standing dream. His odyssey had not been launched for purely intellectual reasons; there were enough men, he felt, in such pursuits already. But Mus had not come so far just to lose his heart to Paris either, and even though he stayed for almost eight years as a student his greatest thrill was his opportunity to depart.

In 1927 Mus was appointed to the prestigious École Française d'Extrême-Orient, the French School of East Asia—an assignment that would take him back to Viet Nam as an archaeologist. With its base in both Hanoi and Paris, the École Française was essentially a research institute engaged with government financing in archaeological exploration and preservation not only in the French colony of Indochina but also throughout Southeast Asia. Under the leadership of the celebrated scholar Georges Coedes, the École Française comprised the largest and most authoritative program of cultural research on the area that has ever existed. The success of its outstanding archaeologists and cultural historians stands as France's greatest enduring achievement in Southeast Asia.

One of Mus's first assignments was to survey the architectural remains of the Kingdom of Champa, which had passed out of existence in the late seventeenth century under relentless battering from the southward expansion of the Vietnamese. Scattered throughout the south-central coastal plain of Viet Nam are dozens of decaying Cham towers and temples that stand forlornly on barren hillocks as if still on guard in defense of their lost kingdom. In recent years these lusterless terra-cotta-colored pylons have found a new vitality as useful reference points for American officers anxious for positions on high ground in their combat around places like Qui Nhon, the Bong Son plain, and Tam Ky. But in the late 1920's the crumbling laterite façades threatened, in their decay, to deny the story of a lost kingdom to those who had survived it. Through his exploration of the ruins Paul Mus began uncovering much of the social history of the Chams and in the process learned for himself of the structural weaknesses in their society which after nearly four centuries of violent conflict with their northern neighbors made them victims of Vietnamese expansion. From this perspective, the time-tested strengths of the Vietnamese stood out and demanded comparisons with the gentle progeny of the earlier conquerors who, in the shadows of crumbling Cham towers, tended their fields routinely.

Recognition of Mus's work among the Cham ruins brought him an unusual opportunity that resulted, several years later, in 1935, in the publication of his most celebrated scholarly study, *Barabudur*. The book was more than just an archaeological treatise about the mammoth temple of a long-dead Hindu kingdom on the Indonesian island of Java. It was also a revealing study of the origins of Buddhism and the role in these origins of antique Southeast Asian kingdoms founded on cultural traditions drawn from India. Although the book was more than a thousand pages (Mus swears, puckishly, that he had the printer put a handful of naughty words in the latter portions just to test those having knowing, yet uninformed, comments on the book's quality), it quickly established his reputation among professionals as a front-ranked scholar on Buddhism and Southeast Asian culture.

Honors and advancement came in the wake of this acclaim over his intellectual brilliance and achievement. Yet such enviable distinction, coming while he was still only in his early thirties, was, for Mus, tinged with a sense of misgiving. During the arduous years of his research, the abortive uprisings of the early 1930's had been launched by incipient revolutionary groups in Viet Nam. For the first time in his life Mus realized that his passionate quest for an understanding of the architectural antiquities of the land and their relationship to the rhythm of life of the rural people was causing him to miss a vital element in Vietnamese society—the spirit of the young revolutionaries.

Mus's most intimate friends among his generation of young Vietnamese were either the privileged upper class with their Parisian education or the rustic people of the countryside. He had simply not been exposed extensively to the groups in between, from which most of the new revolutionaries were emerging. In a vain effort to make contact with this new pulse of Vietnamese life, he awkwardly overlooked a certain Vo Nguyen Giap—the victorious general at Dien Bien Phu in 1954 and now commander of all Vietnamese forces under Hanoi's control—who was, in the early 1930's, a student of the geographer Pierre Gourou, Mus's close friend and colleague. Mus did not seek out those just emerging from the revolutionary influence of French schools, but concentrated on arranging a rendezvous with the more celebrated, though still shadowy, revolutionary figure known to the police as Nguyen Ai Quoc, or "Nguyen the Patriot." But before he could go very far with his scheme, the threatening clouds of war in Europe called him back to France in the more utilitarian role of artillery officer.

Mus's career on the Belgian frontier was, like that of French resistance to the German invasion, brief. In the dismaying aftermath of the fall of France, the thirty-eight-year-old archaeologist-scholar-turned-artillery-commander joined in the desperate optimism of the Free French movement under the promising leadership of General de Gaulle. With the retreat from France, Mus followed the Senegalese artillerymen he had commanded in war to the peaceful capital of their colonial homeland, Dakar, on Africa's eastern tip. Here at a quiet sanctuary away from the dangers of combat the Free French sought a hiatus to repair the disarray in their ranks.

The months of waiting were a catalytic time for Mus. Questions of politics confronted him so completely—the war, the fall of France, the incomprehensible brutality of the Nazis—that he was forced to think about them more seriously than he ever had before. His thoughts, understandably, turned to those issues and people he knew best. Along with others, he sensed that mobilizing the resources of French colonies for the wartime effort would, especially if the war were prolonged, heighten already aroused political expectations among colonial peoples. If such intensified feelings were not anticipated, the restlessness of these peoples seemed certain to come to the surface after the war. Mus, of course, had no special prescience in these matters; he was, after all, not an experienced political analyst. But now perhaps for the first time he suddenly realized that the inevitable path before him included the complex task of piecing together his knowledge of the culture of tropical people with his first intimations about their quest for power and status.

When, finally, after months of waiting, he was chosen to become the Free French representative in the British equivalent of the American O.S.S. (Office of Strategic Services), an espionage and intelligence unit, his transition into the uncertain, kaleidoscopic world of political action entered its most fascinating stage. From Dakar he was sent to Calcutta, his mission unknown. First came a grueling schedule of training, designed to give him the indispensable skills of his new vocation. He learned to make parachute drops, to operate secret radios, to make intelligence estimates, and to survive while making his way through the jungle—a skill that was to prove the handiest of all. Gradually it came to him, though none of his superiors told him (he was still a captain at this point). He was the *one,* the one *they* had chosen. It seemed silly and unbelievable at first. As he got used to the idea, however, he felt rather flattered. Then he wondered if it might not be a mischievous trick of someone who held a secret grudge against him. But it *was* true.

He would drop into Japanese-occupied Indochina, confirm as best he could the estimates of Japanese military strength there, and, while posing as a member of the Nazi-backed Vichy administration left in place by the occupiers, determine the willingness of Frenchmen as well as Vietnamese in the colony to launch a resistance movement that might tie down Japanese forces in the event of an allied landing. Mus's assignment was as seminal as it was uncertain. He was being sent to reconnoiter a wartime situation in Indochina so filled with contradictions and full of explosive potential that it demanded more detailed intelligence. When his parachute opened on a cool moonless, tropical night in late January, 1945, thousands of feet above the jungle canopy of a remote area of Indochina, Mus could hardly have known, as he floated gently downward, back to the familiar land, that he was entering the most convulsive year in Viet Nam's convulsive twentieth century: 1945 was clearly the country's decisive turning point.

Years later, after World War II, an intense, long-smoldering disagreement among "old Indochina hands" over the events of 1945 burst out into public. Hints of the controversy had, of course, been carried widely in the press. But with the publication in 1949 of the memoirs of Admiral Jean Decoux, the Vichy-sponsored wartime Governor General of Indochina, the lines of conflict were revealed more acutely. In effect, Decoux blamed the Free French involvement in Indochina for the successful launching of the revolutionary independence movement in Viet Nam. If the Free French had not pushed their cavalier plans for an improbable "resistance" then, the Admiral asserted, the Japanese would not have been provoked to overturn the Decoux administration, and at war's end Indochina would still have been in French hands. The Viet Minh revolutionaries would, he believed, never have gotten the chance to seize power, and the war in Viet Nam, which for Americans at least still drags on, would have been avoided. Instead, on March 9, 1945, the Japanese, fearful of continued French autonomy in the colony, caught the Decoux regime by surprise in a lightning coup. Virtually all its officials, except for some military units in remote locations, were arrested. Never again would France have effective control over all of Indochina.

Deftly, Paul Mus, in Hanoi at the time of the Japanese coup, escaped from the city of his boyhood and, eluding enemy patrols, made his way through the jungle-covered border country into the sanctuary of China. But he did not escape the strong reproach of Admiral Decoux, who in his memoir reserved some of his most caustic words for what he regarded as Mus's threat to create "anarchy" and "confusion" through his effort to establish a "Committee for the Liberation of Indochina." In a meeting the two men had in late February, 1945, in Hanoi the Admiral records that he reminded Mus of his inexperience in politics and chastised him severely for undermining the legal government in Indochina by his actions. Despite Decoux's understandable harsh feelings (he was imprisoned by the Japanese and considered rather spineless by the French) the demise of his colonial regime in Indochina was due less to the belated and unsuccessful effort to create a "resistance" than it was to Japanese decisions affected by impending defeat and their own brief flirtation with a strategy of guerrilla resistance in Viet Nam. And Mus's mission was obviously not the cavalier escapade Decoux thought it. Mus was, in fact, carrying out the orders of General De Gaulle, who feared that if France did nothing to help liberate Indochina then the allies, especially Roosevelt, would put the colony under an international trusteeship after the war.

In his flight from the Japanese on the night of March 9, Mus had more to worry about than Decoux's future reproaches. Although panic never overtook him, he was deeply perplexed over what attitude the village people in the Red River Delta surrounding Hanoi would take toward his pleas for shelter. Would they aid him in making his escape? Without them he might be lost. Certainly they would not turn their back on someone who knew them so well. Would they turn him over to the Japanese patrols? Or would they simply remain passive, neither helping nor hindering, leaving him instead to his own ingenuity in devising a means of escape? Or was it just possible that they would welcome him as a compatriot and, through that informal network of the country people, speed him on his way. None of these. Their attitude was a surprise. And yet, as the novelty of the situation subsided, Mus chided himself for not at first predicting their response.

The peasants of the delta would help him escape all right. But it was a paternalistic gesture, and though they were not discourteous, they took care to make him aware of it. Even in the most remote villages, the peasants knew that the positions of power in Indochina were now reversed. Their prescience and self-confidence made them seem like a company of actors suddenly adapting to new roles in a new play even though their previous production closed only the night before. This was not a time for revenge. It was simply a time to remind Frenchmen that the Vietnamese have a sense of order of things which often expresses itself in a sudden and complete change of mind. Such change is, for them, inevitable; it occurs in response to a power greater than men. It is a tide running in the affairs of men which reaches its flood and then recedes. It is natural. It is, the Vietnamese believe, heaven. And when the will of heaven is expressed then men must adapt; they must synchronize anew their movement, their lives, to a new order. There is no compulsion—they simply assume their role in a new drama. Nineteen forty-five was a time of such change. For decades the Vietnamese had acquiesced to French rule despite its vulnerabilities. Now the vulnerabilities were exposed for all to see and the acquiescence had come to an end. Frenchmen would not believe it. They would try to restore their rule with the same increments of power (troops, police, administrators) they had before 1945, but it wouldn't work. The French would blame outside influences for their agony but the cause would lie in the mind of the people.

Paul Mus was probably the first Frenchman to experience this change of mind directly. As he made his way from village to village in his escape westward out of the delta into the mountainous Black River country and, finally, to a secret rendezvous with a waiting airplane in the remote, scarcely known, upland valley of Dien Bien Phu, he slowly realized what he was witnessing. He knew intimately, of course, of the time-worn Vietnamese traditions of politics, especially the concept of the Mandate of Heaven, which provided the rationale for the overthrow of one dynasty and its replacement by another. But he thought these notions had passed from the villagers' consciousness along with the demise, under French rule, of their country's monarchy. From his career he was, however, well aware of the continued liveliness of persisting traditions in the cultural life of Vietnamese villages, but it had never occurred to him that these traditions would so completely structure their attitudes toward contemporary politics. What other values, though, did they have to draw upon? And since these persisting traditional values included a sense of belonging to a larger community than the village . . . Now it began to come clear.

But when he tried to explain to French officials in Chungking that the Vietnamese peasants had sensed a change in the Mandate of Heaven and were awaiting a sign of a new order in the country, they dismissed him with amusement. He was still trying to explain when in late August, 1945, the Viet Minh took over Hanoi and Ho Chi Minh proclaimed the independence of Viet Nam.

The sudden appearance of a well-organized revolutionary government in Hanoi was, however, hardly a surprise to the French. In fact, as late as mid-August, 1945, clandestine French intelligence teams, along with their American O.S.S. counterparts, were at the remote mountain command post of the small nucleus of the future revolutionary government trying to persuade its leaders to carry out guerrilla raids against the Japanese. Shrewdly, the Viet Minh, as the revolutionary movement was known, played off both sides in the war to gain weapons and a favorable political position.

In critical sequence, the Viet Minh received 5,000 American arms parachuted into their mountain redoubt. With the added boldness these weapons stimulated, they marched into Hanoi, where they cajoled from the Japanese the major part of captured French arsenals. Despite their political finesse, the French still did not regard the Viet Minh as a very substantial force in Vietnamese politics. Their "successes" were attributed to the lack of any opposition—an analysis which conveniently led to the conclusion that once France returned in force politics in Indochina would be put in its proper perspective. Perhaps a few concessions would be necessary to mollify the Viet Minh, but there was nothing in their adventures to suggest, to French eyes at least, any fundamental changes that would prevent a timely restoration of colonial rule.

Paul Mus, when he returned to Viet Nam in September, 1945, as a political adviser to General Philippe Leclerc, the humble, heroic liberator of Paris and the commander of French reoccupation forces in Indochina, was a man destined to be caught between French illusions and Vietnamese revolution. Happily, Mus's first superior, General Leclerc, was not possessed by the illusion that Western military force could indefinitely control an Asian peasant society. Leclerc's emphasis on negotiations with the Viet Minh was founded on his shrewd assessment that France simply did not have the military resources sufficient to subdue a Vietnamese population risen up against it. His estimate was not based on a knowledge of Vietnamese society—that's why he relied upon Mus. But few men knew the limits of available military resources better than Leclerc, since he had been responsible for organizing them for the liberation of a now war-ravaged France. Repeatedly, he warned that a military response to the revolutionary movement in Viet Nam, though it might succeed in controlling the cities, would merely drive the Viet Minh into an almost limitless sanctuary of bamboo-screened villages in the Vietnamese countryside, where they would, through their scattered guerrilla raids, be impossible to control or, perhaps, even to negotiate with.

Early one mid-December evening in 1946, after nearly a year of fruitless negotiations that were filled with haggling, often undermined, and never supplied with an atmosphere of trust or a spirit of purpose, the Viet Minh, sensing a slow erosion in their position of strength, struck out at the French in Hanoi and other major towns in northern Viet Nam. Although after these pre-emptive blows portions of the Viet Minh units held out against the French for almost a month, they were a diversion. That same December night the main body slipped out of the cities under the cover of darkness and made their way to prearranged base areas in the deltas and mountains surrounding the towns. Leclerc's worst fears had been realized. The pattern of conflict that emerged—predicted by Leclerc with chilling accuracy—still exists between urban governments and the people of the countryside.

The showdown in Viet Nam produced in France in 1947 two sharply contrasting public outcries—one of wrath and one of dismay—similar to yet less intense than those in the United States in February, 1965. The wrathful wanted to "teach the perfidious Vietnamese a lesson," while the dismayed anxiously demanded negotiations with the Viet Minh to head off what they feared would be a needlessly tragic colonial war. As a sop to its public, the French government—so hopelessly divided at home that it could not control the provocations of its representatives in Indochina—dispatched a new set of officials to the colony. Of only slightly less inflexibility than their predecessors, these men realized that they could not compromise with the Viet Minh and still expect to have much prospect for their political careers in France. Perhaps they knew deep down that it was all an illusion, that France really couldn't subdue the Viet Minh, that Leclerc was right, but it was an illusion that had the power of reality. France was too unsure of itself at home to risk a blow to its prestige from Vietnamese guerrillas. The colonial mystique was too inextricably wound up with what France thought itself to be; decolonization was an issue most politicians wanted to defer. Although a policy of force was never really in doubt, symbolic gestures of compromise had to be found both to mollify left-wing opinion in France and to demonstrate Viet Minh intransigence in Viet Nam.

Paul Mus became that symbolic gesture. He would be sent into the Vietnamese countryside by himself, without diplomatic immunity or military escort, in search of Ho Chi Minh. When he found the Viet Minh leader, Mus was authorized to present verbally the conditions under which the French High Commissioner would agree to a cease-fire and a new set of negotiations. Mus could not enter into any bargaining himself. His message was to be presented on a take-it-or-leave-it basis. Since the terms he carried called for the Viet Minh to lay down their arms and regroup in easily contained perimeters, the response of Ho Chi Minh, if Mus ever saw him, was virtually assured. If the Viet Minh either by accident or outrage were to kill Mus, then the High Commissioner would have a convenient martyr whose death he could justifiably avenge. If, on the other hand, Ho Chi Minh were to accept the terms—so much the better. But if he acted predictably and rejected them, then the High Commissioner would have clean hands as the inevitable military campaign began against the Vietnamese countryside.

As Mus left the French sanctuary of Hanoi in early May, 1947, to venture into the countryside alone by foot in search of Ho Chi Minh, the contrasts with his previous flight from the city in 1945, though deeply troubling, gave him a feeling of amused satisfaction. The situations were reversed the way he sensed they would be. In escaping from the Japanese, the countryside had been a place of sanctuary to hide from capture, but now it exposed him and there was no place to hide from the searching eyes of the village people as he passed by. In 1945 they had been looking for a sign of a new order, and when Ho Chi Minh emerged to proclaim the independence of Viet Nam the suddenness and lack of opposition merely confirmed to them, in the apparent effortlessness of the act, that it was a sign of heaven. Not every one of them was, in 1947, already a member of the Viet Minh—far from it. They knew there would be a time of flux as the new order took form. But each of them seemed to reflect, in their knowing glances at Mus as he trudged onward, the awareness that the Viet Minh leadership had joined with them in the countryside. The feeling of community they sought, which would give them once again a status recognized beyond the village and therefore a sense of harmony with the land, the sky, and each other, was beginning.

When he reached the Viet Minh redoubt in the mountainous fringe of the Red River Delta, Mus was exhausted; he had walked almost forty miles over neglected roads and the frail dikes of rice fields and he had had no rest. He had walked past Hanoi's outer defense perimeter dotted with vulnerable watchtowers, entering the no man's land where French authority did not extend and finally into the Viet Minh zone. In agreeing to the mission he knew it would be arduous and dangerous. It was not the first time he had undertaken such a risky operation. He knew that he might be killed and he knew also that he was being used by French officialdom to the possible detriment of his own career. It was obvious that Ho Chi Minh could not accept the terms being brought to him, and if Mus attempted, without authorization, to bargain with Ho, the terms he might bring back to Hanoi would make him appear as an advocate of the Viet Minh cause in French councils. His chances of advancement, perhaps even to Minister of Overseas France (a new name for the old Minister of Colonies), a possibility often spoken of in the postwar years, would be harmed, perhaps irreparably, by a risky identification with the anticolonial cause. Yet he willingly accepted the task, despite the affrontery of the terms he carried, because he hoped Ho Chi Minh would suggest some new way to avert a bitter and prolonged war. Perhaps he was politically naïve; he wouldn't disagree with such an opinion.

But there are times, he felt, when a man must do some things or he can no longer believe in himself.

It was well past midnight when Mus was finally led into the Viet Minh headquarters; overcome with fatigue he fell immediately to sleep. When they woke him he was momentarily disoriented; it was still dark and he was uncertain why he had been wakened. The luminous dial of his watch said it was three o'clock. The leader, Ho Chi Minh, was ready to receive him, they said. He splashed water on his face and followed quickly along, smiling in realization that Ho was giving him no advantages. They ushered him into a shadowy candlelit room, and from behind a rough table a familiar bone-thin man in a drab tunic emerged from out of the half darkness. There was on his face a whimsical smile and quizzical flashing eyes punctuated above by highly arched brows and a stringy-thin beard below. He motioned for Mus to sit opposite him; alone the two men hunched over the shadowy table as if locked in a game of chess.

He had heard that Mus wanted to discuss his appeal for a cease-fire. Did Mus have some written proposal from the High Commissioner? What terms could he offer? What authorization to enter into discussions did he have? Slowly, hesitantly, Mus related to him the list of nonnegotiable demands which the High Commissioner wished conveyed as a response to his cease-fire appeal. The Viet Minh were being asked to lay down their arms and, in effect, permit the French to consolidate their control over the country. Mus tried to phrase these harsh terms in as detached tones as possible in hopes that he might elicit some promising counterproposal. This was the one good card Mus had to play in the deepening tragedy of Viet Nam and he wanted it to count, to make a difference.

When Mus had finished, Ho Chi Minh abruptly turned the conversation to a chatty, almost leisurely review of the events of the past several years, particularly the attempt by France to form a commonwealth with its colonies, which it called the French Union. If it were to become a reality, he mused at length, such a Union would have to be founded on principles of mutual respect and dignity. Then suddenly, after what had seemed like an hour-long interlude, he confronted Mus forcefully, his eyes flashing in cadence with the flickering candlelight, and said in emphatic understatement, "In the French Union there is no place for cowards; if I accept these terms, I would be one." The meeting was over. Ho motioned Mus to leave the room and ordered his men to bid him depart for Hanoi as the first light of a new day was dawning among the hills of Viet Nam.

Making his way back to Hanoi, Mus was hardly aware of his fatigue or of the danger of being mistaken as an intruder and shot. His disappointment was greater than his fatigue, and he was so lost in thought about the significance of the meeting just ended that he forgot about the dangers. When he reached Hanoi's outer perimeter and was challenged by French patrols, he realized suddenly why he knew, unconsciously, that his return would be safe. The Viet Minh control over the area he had passed through was based on something other than force, something that assured his safety. It was this something, predictable on the basis of his knowledge of Viet Nam, that he had been thinking about while stumbling back, head down, to Hanoi, knowing all the time that he would be safe.

All of his adult years, Mus had devoted himself to the study of peasant life in Viet Nam and adjacent countries. He had been in search of a childhood dream which he thought, correctly, would give greater continuity and richer meaning to his life. His odyssey, now leading him back to the French enclave of Hanoi, had been based on the belief that there is a rhythm to the life of peasants synchronized around the cycle of growing rice in irrigated fields. And in this rhythm, reflected as it was in the delicate forms of decaying monuments, he felt there was a lesson to be learned about the cohesiveness of life. Mus had explained these lessons in scholarly writing; Ho Chi Minh had put them into action as political power.

The meeting in the Viet Minh mountain redoubt had not been their first. Mus had seen Ho several times during the preceding year of fruitless negotiations, mainly in Hanoi. What a surprise it had been to learn that Ho Chi Minh was in fact the Nguyen Ai Quoc who Mus and the French Sûreté had been so anxious to find in the 1930's! But as he had gotten to know Ho Chi Minh an even greater revelation was the striking parallels in the two men's careers. Although Ho was a revolutionary and Mus a scholar, they had both been looking for the same thing, but for entirely different reasons, of course. Ho's search for the secret of the strength and the cohesiveness in Viet Nam's peasant society was a quest for power to overthrow French rule and make the country united and independent. He found this secret in the peasant's continuing sense of belonging to a larger community beyond the village. By using old, persisting concepts, he created the framework for a new spirit of community based on totally new values. His purpose was to link the villagers to a new sense of Viet Nam as a nation by making their traditions relevant to participation in the modern politics of revolution. Instead of the extremely limited participation in politics characteristic of Viet Nam's Confucian kingdoms, Ho wanted mass involvement, and to get it he had to persuade villagers to accept new values by linking them to familiar traditions.

Mus's mission had convinced him of two things: of Ho's great confidence in the Viet Minh's revolutionary program and of the success of this program in the countryside through which he had passed. French forces might well reoccupy these regions, but they would not be able to establish any dependable means of exercising authority over them. The peasants would be rice farmers innocently working their fields by day but at night they would become local guerrillas dedicated to sabotage and to the support of Viet Minh regular forces by stocking caches of food and weapons. They had accepted a new form of authority—one which did not have to protect them against the French to maintain their confidence. Cut off by French occupation of their local area they would still be loyal to the revolutionary cause and perform the valuable task of wearing away at the enemy's rear areas. The Viet Minh would be everywhere because the people were everywhere. There would be no battlefronts and there would be no massed formations to fight with the French over control of territory. This would be a war for the people and not for control over the land. And somehow Mus felt he must do something more to avert it before it went further.

But he couldn't. Not really. Yet he tried. He tried to be a mediator in the higher echelons of the French establishment in Viet Nam, but his efforts had little effect. Like the Americans after them, there was only one way for the French to rid themselves of illusions about the effectiveness of force in continuing their influence in Viet Nam. Use it. Commit troops, firepower, and prestige. See them consumed in a continuing struggle in which there was no way to turn military force into political authority without creating a bond of community with those in the countryside. Despite the bloodshed and frustration of a quarter of a century, no one of influence would ever think much about the needs for political community in Viet Nam, and if he did, he would never advance a program for creating it.

No one, that is, except the Vietnamese revolutionaries, and they, of course, have been led by the Communists. And that is what has bothered most people who ever thought about Viet Nam. Why was it that the Communists could instill such great discipline and sacrifice in the Vietnamese they led and why, at the same time, couldn't the anti-Communists? Paul Mus had answers to such questions, but his official colleagues were too preoccupied with the immediacy of operations and too sure that all Mus would offer would be compromise and further negotiations to give much credence to his ideas. So finally, reluctantly, Mus left Viet Nam rather than stand by helplessly on the sidelines while the land of his youth was destroyed in a war between his fellow Frenchmen and his fellow Vietnamese.

When he returned to France, Paul Mus decided that he must try to present his ideas to the French people in hopes that a change in public opinion would have an effect in restraining officials in Viet Nam from following a policy of force. He wrote numerous articles for popular journals, among them the prestigious Paris daily *Le Monde,* and in 1952 he published a lengthy book called *Viet Nam: sociologie d'une guerre*, which was hailed in intellectual circles but had little impact on governmental leaders. Perhaps it was too late in appearing. After all, by 1952 even "tough-minded" politicians were sick of the war in Viet Nam and were anxious to find some face-saving way out of it. They were not particularly interested in understanding Vietnamese politics or the necessary requirements for a durable peace in the country; they simply wanted to be rid of Viet Nam. In many ways the attitude in France at that time resembles the mood in America as the 1970's begin. Perhaps Americans, less used to adversity than the French, are so sick of Viet Nam that they really don't want to hear about it any more either. But, perhaps also, there are Americans who sense that even with America out of the country, Viet Nam will continue to be at war with itself over the constitution of political power in its society and, therefore, a microcosm of what is happening in much of the world as peasant people grope for modern lives.

This prologue introduces a book based on Mus's writings in the late 1940's and early 1950's after his return from Viet Nam. The book is an effort to put in concise and readable form the essence of his insights into Vietnamese character and the nature of revolution in Viet Nam. Although Paul Mus gave his approval and cooperation in the preparation of the book he is in no way responsible for its shortcomings. Many readers who know of his writings in French may well be disturbed that a particularly favorite article or chapter of theirs was not included here. They should not blame Paul Mus, because he did not select the pieces to be included nor did he organize the substantive presentation or make stylistic changes in the way his ideas were rendered into English. The book is, therefore, the sole responsibility of his American collaborator, a former student, who chose the materials, adapted them for English-language readers by completely reorganizing the presentation of his ideas and revising the style in which they were written, and prepared the prologue and epilogue. This transformation seemed desirable both because of the difficulties of a direct translation and the rather complex style with which many of the ideas were originally presented in French, as well as the datedness of some portions and the great length of the whole.

The purpose of this book is not to discuss every aspect of a quarter of a century of revolution in Viet Nam. Its only purpose is to discuss the most essential missing aspect of this revolution in the public debate over the conflict during the past twenty-five years: the underlying attitudes and values of the Vietnamese peasants, why they have been unwilling to accept the legitimacy of pro-French and pro-American urban-based governments, and why they have steadily moved toward the Communist-led revolutionaries in every area of Viet Nam. After an initial chapter analyzing the effects of French colonialism on the traditional political organization of Viet Nam, there are two chapters that discuss in depth the essential persisting qualities of this tradition in the minds of the Vietnamese peasants. Then there is a chapter which sets forth some of the requirements for creating a modern state in Viet Nam, followed by a discussion of how France provided some but not all of these needs for modernization and in the process caused new tensions in the society. Next there is a description of the formation of the pro-French elite in Viet Nam and a searching analysis of why they have been unable to provide leadership for rural Vietnamese. Then come two chapters which show how Marxism has been adapted to the needs of Vietnamese society by the Communist revolutionary leadership. And finally, there is an analysis of some of the prospects for modernization in Viet Nam, followed by a summary epilogue.

Underlying this discussion and analysis there are some general assumptions about the nature of revolution. Revolution is many things, but primarily it is a question of power—how power is to be organized in a society, who is to have it, and how they are to get it. Because power cannot be held effectively or predictably without being institutionalized into authority, a word used to convey the legitimate use of power, revolution is also a crisis of legitimacy which focuses around two main issues: (1) the capacity of institutions to get compliance with their decisions and (2) the political status of individuals. Any decline in compliance with governmental decisions is most often ascribed to an erosion in legitimacy, and explanations are sought in changed attitudes about the status of individuals vis-à-vis a government. Such explanations point up the belief that power is held on the basis of values shared by both the governed and the governors. Paul Mus's contribution is to show why revolution in Viet Nam is a crisis of values—values around which people organize their lives and gauge their expectations about the treatment they will get from governments. Because values have not changed rapidly in Viet Nam, revolution continues, and it continues to follow patterns which have repeated themselves in a struggle that will undoubtedly persist until there is some resolution about the values on which power will be organized in Viet Nam.

I.

Viet Nam: A Nation Off Balance

The bitter fighting in Viet Nam is a constant reminder that what takes place in that far-off corner of Asia concerns the whole world, whose fate is to some extent being decided there. Viet Nam lies between China, where nearly a quarter of the earth's population is already Communist, and India, where nearly another quarter of the earth's population still shares the political philosophy of the West, and yet Western nations are in general ignorant of the country. That ignorance is no small part of the problem.

Realizing their ignorance, neutral observers from many nations have gone to Viet Nam to see it for themselves. Their visits are critical, quite apart from the war, for the reports these observers send back will have political significance for a long time to come. On the basis of such impressions, nations will form their policies toward Viet Nam. And since the relations between two countries are always influenced by what each one believes the other thinks of her, the judgments these visitors form on the spot will affect politics twice—in their own countries and in Viet Nam itself. The Vietnamese are observing the observers.

The first reactions of these observers have long since appeared. Like many others before them, they are charmed by the character and spirit of the Vietnamese people. When criticism is offered it is aimed at Vietnamese society, or—more accurately—at the alleged

---

This chapter appeared in a slightly different version in *The Yale Review,* vol. XLI (Summer 1952), pp. 524–533. It appears here by permission of the managing editor of the *Review.*

Vietnamese incapacity for forming a society, at their excessive individualism.

"They expect a lot from other people, especially from the French and the Americans, but they are not inclined to assume much responsibility themselves. They break their word unless they see some immediate advantage in keeping it; they fail to understand the importance of a lofty and scrupulous morality in social and business relationships. They have no team spirit, no long-range plans. It's every man for himself, and the only disgrace is to be found out." Such description is a common refrain in most reports with a Saigon dateline.

No civic spirit, a general lack of foresight, the individual disengaged and alienated from society—such is the dark side of the picture drawn by visitors to Viet Nam. They give us another side, too, but the dark side is worth emphasizing because it presents the most problems, especially the problem of accounting for these faults. Are they to be attributed to some profound lack in the Vietnamese character, or to the way circumstances have shaped Vietnamese life, or to some peculiarity in the attitude of the observers, undoubtedly men of good will?

Often, it is true, the good and bad qualities observed seem to cancel each other out. The visitors have not overlooked the tremendous activity of the Vietnamese in all their undertakings, or the often astonishing ingenuity they display in performing the tasks of daily life. Stories are told of their devoted friendships, of their profound feeling for family solidarity. Can all this be true of a people without community spirit? Can the Vietnamese be considered the victims of collective apathy at the very moment when the energy and tenacity of their troops, including those of the Communist-led revolutionaries that fought so well against France and now fight against the United States, command the attention of the world? The late French General de Lattre de Tassigny paid tribute to the mettle of the troops he faced in personal circumstances that rendered his homage moving.

Yet the contradictions do exist; in fact, at present the Vietnamese seem to be made of contradictions. But this is an accident of the historical moment; it is not inherent in their nature. Long acquaintance with the Vietnamese reveals that they have abundant group spirit, not only in their family life but also in their village communities, the touchstone of their traditional society. It is from these villages that any real interpretation of Viet Nam must take its point of departure.

Traditional Concepts of Political Community

The typical village of Viet Nam is enclosed within a thick wall of bamboo and thorny plants; the villagers used to live behind a kind of screen of bamboo, or perhaps it was more like living within the magic ring of a fairy tale. Supplying their needs from the surrounding fields, they kept to themselves behind their common protection, away from strangers, away, even, from the state. For instance, when it came to taxes (there, as elsewhere, the state's chief concern) they still presented a united front. They paid their taxes as a group, and the community was responsible. The villages dominated the landscape; they were the backbone of the nation. Yet each preserved an internal autonomy, and autarchy, with an economy based on local consumption. Before the Europeans arrived, the Chinese carried on what commerce there was.

The traditional Vietnamese state was conventionalized in accordance with Confucian political thought; it was withdrawn behind a wall of Chinese characters. It was authoritarian, but it preserved a ritualistic distance between itself and its subjects. At the same time it intervened directly in village life by regulating the agricultural calendar and by imposing, through its rituals, attitudes and standards of deportment upon the group and the individual. By its right of inspection of village affairs the state guaranteed conformity to the models provided by Chinese tradition; the codifications of the Le dynasty, in the fifteenth century, are an outstanding example.

The traditional Vietnamese state kept its budgetary requirements to a minimum by governing through powers of verification and eventual repression, but not of execution. The responsibility for detailed implementation remained with the villages. The state was a coordinator, not an executive. Its object was to prevent the smaller communities from going astray, and its chief "ministers" (the word does not have its European meaning) were a kind of high tribunal sitting in judgment upon lapses from the Confucian model. Therefore, the state recruited its personnel for all but the humblest positions from the literati, whose learning consisted entirely of Confucius, the classics, and their commentators.

China provided a description of this sort of system in a rich collection of writings and exegeses. Society was the content of its own literature, and that was what it expected of itself. To say that the education of the officials was literary is also to say that it was in some sense social, but it was not oriented toward the future, as Western social studies are. There was interest in ameliorating the present, to be sure, but the ideal to be achieved lay in the past. Since present evils resulted from neglect of the Confucian model, their cure lay not in innovation but in return to the ideal. Knowledge as social technique was pure conformism.

Such an attitude had far-reaching consequences. It made for a relatively inexpensive state, with no need to impose crushing taxes on the villages; but in the end its thrift came dear, because, by renouncing the idea of constructive progress and by a civic orientation different from ours, the traditional system of politics in Viet Nam was fragile indeed against the shock of the modern world. Looking forward to no future that was not a repetition of a better past, the state could not on principle delegate any new authority to its citizens. By contrast, the Western state seeks constantly to engage the attention of the citizen, because it expects to find progress in something new; we need representative institutions to assure the participants and taxpayers that the solution reached is a step forward, the best thing that could be done. But when all wisdom, every solution there is to be found, already exists in the past, then—if everything in the state is going well in other respects —"book learning" is sufficient to guide the mandarin of a district.

In the rustic village communities of Viet Nam a representative body was certainly useful, but its object was not an equalitarian vote. Rather, it expressed the hierarchical structure of society. Age, literary accomplishments, and to a lesser degree the accumulation of wealth provided the basis of the hierarchy. Family relationships counted, too; the head of a family intervened and accounted for his descendants and dependents.

Historically the chief danger to such a system is that a parasitic aristocracy could establish itself by annexing the political offices and accumulating great estates, with the real workers falling to the level of serfs, as in all other agricultural countries. But this could not happen in Viet Nam because the emperor never granted permanent titles. The entailed estates were always ritualistic and symbolic, bound to the family altar. As for the grades in the administrative bureaucracy, or mandarinate, as it was called by Europeans, which formed the true hierarchy of the country, they were open to public competition and thus theoretically accessible to everyone. The cities were very slightly developed and commercial privileges had been practically monopolized by the Chinese, discouraging the accumulation of large urban fortunes, which were very vulnerable to reprisal and confiscation by the central power anyway.

In the villages, as elsewhere, custom did not favor large landholding. The land was split up in parcels, often very small, at least in the rice-growing areas, which are the heart of the country. To accumulate even a modest estate was the work of a lifetime, and no family could stay at the top in one of the little villages for very long. Prestige was expensive; its obligations served as an economic leveler, since society gauged prestige by the fulfillment of those obligations. Parties, banquets, and subscriptions were ways for the rest of the people in the community to share the wealth of whoever had reached social eminence. A popular proverb from China summarized the situation: "Nobody stays rich for three generations; nobody stays poor for three generations." It is characteristic of village life that the proverb has meaning only when "nobody" is understood to mean "no *family*"; the individual is but a momentary phenomenon.

From various sources we know what products were exported from Indochina back in the seventeenth century, when there began to be a sizable trade with Europe. Few of them came from the Vietnamese countryside, with its economy based on local consumption. They came instead from the highlands of the country with their lacquer trees and their mulberry trees, or from the wooded mountains and foothills, peopled by non-Vietnamese, especially by the mountain Tai and Muongs, who lived between the Thais of Thailand and the Vietnamese. In getting these products to the coast and its junks, the Chinese were the middlemen. The government confined its activities to levying customs.

The traditional state did, however, assume one other major function, which contributed at least as much to its authority as its ritualistic aspect did, and more concretely: the military function. Viet Nam did not just happen; she occupied her territory only at the price of incessant wars. When, in 939, she at last freed herself from more than ten centuries of Chinese domination, she found herself engaged in a war to the death with her neighbor to the south, the Hindu Kingdom of Champa, which then occupied the seacoast of modern Viet Nam from north of Dong Hoi to south of Nha Trang. It took centuries to bring their occupation to an end; only a little before their final defeat in 1470–71 (after which they more or less disappeared except for small conclaves around the coastal town of Phan Rang) they were still waging war on Vietnamese territory.

The vigor with which the army defended the country can be judged from the fact that in the thirteenth century it defeated the redoubtable Mongol invaders who raised such havoc in Europe. It also organized the territory behind the front of its advances. As it conquered the land it established a network of military villages or villages of veterans, then a penal colony, especially suitable for political exiles, and finally a solid blanket of free villages of the ordinary sort. This is what happened, for instance, in southern Viet Nam (what the Vietnamese call Nam Bo and was once known as "French Cochin China"). The army's work was an irreversible process, beyond temporary military reversals. Because of it, the Chams, who won many battles, lost the war and—even more—lost the peace. The army led the Vietnamese peasants (which is to say Viet Nam itself) clear down to the Gulf of Siam, and today the Chams of Annam and the Cambodians of Cochin China survive only in books and in their beautiful Hindu art in the museums.

Besides these foreign wars, which formed the basis of national development, there were bitter civil conflicts between north and south in the seventeenth and eighteenth centuries. At that time the military forces seem to have been complemented by a police apparatus especially developed in the chief cities. The ritualistic state was neither withdrawn nor a sluggard in those days.

European experts who have had an opportunity to examine the budgets of traditional Viet Nam have been struck by their modesty. As far as possible the policy of governmental decentralization resulted in public works being located near the villages that would build them and benefit from them. From on high the state coordinated these collective works or decided that they should be undertaken, but the works themselves were the product of local participation. Each village built and maintained its own section of a dike, dug its own portion of a canal. Each raised its own contingent of recruits for the imperial army and took care of its supplies. Since taxes were levied largely in kind, there did not have to be enough money in circulation to encroach upon village autonomy.

The political superstructure in the traditional Vietnamese state also followed a policy of social aid. The mandarins kept stores of rice against public calamities, which always threatened in a land where the coast lies open to typhoons and the plains in the river deltas are in danger of periodic floods, though their reserves of food were insufficient for the worst years.

The Impact of French Colonialism on Viet Nam's Political Traditions

This description of traditional Vietnamese life is hardly an account of a school for anarchic individualism, such as some observers think ought to be attributed to Vietnamese life today. Must, then, this deterioration of the national life be set down, in some degree, to more than seventy-five years of French domination? To do so, with due qualification, one need not call the colonial regime pure oppression, as some like to say it was. Would not Vietnamese civic spirit have had sufficient reason for decay in the fact that political life was reduced to a matter of pure administration and that (to make it worse) the administration was in the hands of foreigners? On the other hand, polemicists have a good chance to point out how the framework of village life was struck a body blow by the French conception of taxes, payable in money and levied on a scale that must have seemed exorbitant to the villagers. The traditional village could not survive. It continued to look the same, at least in Tonkin and in Annam (Bac Bo, or northern Viet Nam, and Trung Bo, or central Viet Nam), but it became an empty shell, void of the social substance it had once had which had kept life constantly renewed. With the heart gone out of it, even the appearance of the village was in a precarious position unless there could be a complete reversal in direction, back to the lost equilibrium of life. That is what some have still wished for, but is it possible?

The growth of cities; the extension of an economy based on money listed on the international exchanges; the bonds money has created between city and country, with the resulting usurious loans and accumulation of large landed estates; control by the central administration reaching down into village affairs; the need to secularize the state—all these factors have made the resident, the *dân,* into a taxpayer in the modern sense of the word: one who pays his taxes in money as an individual rather than as part of a collective anonymity who paid taxes in rice or other products. Yet the colonial situation did not permit this evolution to be accompanied and compensated for by what would have made him a citizen of the modern world.

Thus the Confucian balance between the ritualistic state and the autarchic village was brought to ruin, or nearly so, without anything in sight to replace it. Viet Nam still seeks her way amid that ruin. War has aggravated her plight but has not caused it.

There is not necessarily any injustice in admitting that France was never responsive enough to what was required of her in Viet Nam—a country that still does not understand herself, thrown into confusion as she is by a violent change in the direction of her history. Yet to a considerable extent it is what France has done in Viet Nam that makes indispensable—and at the same time possible —what almost all Western countries fail to recognize and still formally refuse to admit: that Viet Nam should be a united and independent nation.

This goal is what the present cleavage and state of war are all about, and the elements for its solution are not local but clearly depend on an international settlement. But first a more modest need must be fulfilled: to set straight the facts about Viet Nam herself. For if these facts can be understood only in relation to the international complications, it is also true that the international aspects of the situation can be understood only if the local aspects are clear.

Freed from French influence, at least in its colonial aspect, Vietnamese historians should no longer consider the century just past as a chapter in the history of French colonialism, but as a chapter in their own history. Seen from that angle, it will seem less an interruption than a preparation for the modern world. Such a transition was and still is a very serious matter, with far-reaching consequences; but it is a Vietnamese, not a colonial, problem. Colonialism has only hastened it.

Some conservatives optimistically see a political, social, and even constabulatory remedy to present troubles in a return to traditional village institutions, more or less brought up to date. There, they say, Viet Nam would once more find her true nature. But such a reversal in the flow of history could be realized only with the greatest difficulty. The lost Confucian equilibrium was a whole, in a vanished world; it cannot be brought back piecemeal, and that world will not return.

The contemporary state is a builder, an entrepreneur, an organizer, an umpire in everyday affairs. It is centralized, as modern action is. A group of villagers can build a dike, but they cannot build a railroad or buy the rolling stock for it. Still less can they cope with the problems of air communication; an airport located near a rural village serves the world. A state which takes charge of such undertakings, in whole or in part, or which has associated with it private interests participating in the national life, is, as far as these enterprises go, irredeemably cut off from the Confucian body. For better or for worse, the civil state, individual responsibility, and heavy taxes are part of the modern fate. To abandon them would be to abandon the economy, and ultimately the politics of the country, not merely to the advice but to the initiative of foreigners. The ritualistic state and the traditional village, with their separation and adjustment, belong to another world.

Viet Nam's lack of balance (insofar as it does not result from the cause most easily recognized, the terrible circumstances of war) comes from the irreparable loss of that ancient harmony which gave to life its sense of being natural. Rather than creating this situation, colonialism disguised it. Any really national government that one can imagine coming to power and being accepted would have had to face the same thing.

It is not surprising that Western observers now report contradictory impressions. They are visiting a land where much has happened in the course of history. Some of the past is still present, though without external sign; some of it has been lost, and the lack of what once was often has more effect than what remains.

Traditional Concepts of Individual Responsibility

Before the colonial period, national custom had shaped Vietnamese life in accordance with two orders of duty. A man's first duty was to the local community, to his family and village, a harmonious whole to which he contributed a single note. But this alone was not enough; man also received from on high a standard of behavior, of attitude, and even of intention, all embodied in traditional rites. The farmers were brought up to believe that the success of their labors and their survival itself depended on ritualistic observations; in this way they won the favor of heaven and assured their harmony with nature. Such was the second order of duty, observed with particular care by people of property. All the glamour and prestige of Chinese civilization guaranteed the authenticity of these two orders of duty, and their compatibility.

The most profound characteristic of such a mentality is that it found itself in balance with its own view of the world. The equivalents of our natural sciences were in that view full of moral and civic values. Chinese learning and politics described a society "according to nature." Everything a man had to do was part of a larger scheme of things, as for our naturalists every individual is part of a genus and species; every duty was, in the full force of the word, natural. Anything that did not belong, that failed to find its rightful place—whether in the state under the sovereign, or in the village with its counsel and guardian spirit, or in the family under its chief—was beyond nature. Whatever it was, it had shunned "the way" (*tao*), the order and law of things, and, escaping morality, became mere gambling with fate.

Thus, mixed in with fully developed institutions and the ordered nature surrounding them was an obscure, disorganized potentiality; its image was the life of the rice growers, whose work was always menaced by a return of disorder, either social or meteorological. The same wisdom that inspired Pascal's "Neither beast nor angel" and the practical social formula of the Hindus (a balance among virtue, profit, and passion) also found expression in Sino-Vietnamese empiricism. It reserved a place for individual or social activities on the fringes of the perfected forms and their rituals. But such ventures lay outside the realm of man's duties; they did not belong to any "natural" relationship; they entered upon an uncharted land. Their only criterion was success.

All this shows why the accounts of the way people comport themselves in Saigon today should not be taken as a guide to Vietnamese character, but as a social sign marking the times. Today, Vietnamese life has broken with its historical sequence. Present behavior would have been out of the question under a stable Confucian government in which an omnipresent morality governed conduct from top to bottom, through all the ranks of natural groups. But even at times when the disorder taking place in the nation and the government may seem entirely external, the confusion in group life deprives ordinary men not only of a material prop but also of a moral code. The groups that determine the individual's outlook have disappeared. It is an interregnum of "natural" society. The individual is left to his own initiative; anything goes. Yet all await indications of a return to normal order.

The structure of Chinese and Vietnamese traditional culture cannot be restored. The conviction that its restoration would be useful is not enough to bring it back. It worked for thousands of years because those who participated in it believed that it was *true*. The unrivaled learning of the Chinese and the prestige of their writings guaranteed its truth, even for those who knew Chinese culture only from afar. Our sciences have destroyed all that, in institutions as well as in absolute values. The ritualistic state has no modern equivalent.

The other basis of traditional morality is hardly better off: village autarchy has been ruined throughout Viet Nam by the contemporary economy, based entirely on exchange. Shaken from above, with the loss of a sovereign power harmonizing with nature, their topmost stay, economic and political institutions collapse from below, with the loss of the ancient economic structure.

The Possibilities for Social Reconstruction

Is there any basis for reconstruction?

The charge to bring against the foreign domination is not that it destroyed time-honored institutions; in so doing the French merely performed a historical function. Besides, they had begun to provide for the country technically, administratively, and by educating a group of leaders—not large enough, to be sure, but of high quality. Their real mistake was that they introduced a monetary economy displacing a barter economy without being sufficiently aware of the need to adjust it to the whole society of the country. It was necessary to bear with the economy already in operation (an economy based upon autonomous villages) for a time, but the object should have been to eliminate it by gradually educating the people of the countryside for something else.

Instead of that progressive policy, the French chose to maintain the old order, with the laudable motive of avoiding any shock to the local social structure, but with the practical result that in the country the economy continued to be based on little trade and local consumption, while in the cities there developed a modern commercial economy based on worldwide exchange. Those who organized trade maintained the workers on the level of the traditional economy but sold the product of their work on the level of the city economy. The difference between the two went into their own pockets.

In short, a copy of the Chinese system of exploitation was grafted onto the country, but with a new occidental twist to it. The difference was that the French had to overcome a distance between the Vietnamese and themselves that did not exist (or at least not to the same degree) between the Vietnamese and the Chinese. The necessary middlemen were furnished by the local community, and they took an increasingly large part in the circulation of money, especially in the cities. Their position allowed them to prime any opposition to the French colonial element. At the same time, by their practice of the traditional usury, favored by the peasant's new need for money, they worked a profound change in Vietnamese society. Here one sees how society can be shaped by taxes when the taxes are modernized before the means of payment are. They cast off its ruling traditions; they went to the cities to live. And those that remained behind carried on their business through Chinese middlemen.

The difference between the two economic systems should have been progressively reduced by educating the peasant masses, but instead it was stabilized, making things very convenient for the middlemen.

The adjustment that faces any national government of the new Viet Nam is a fundamental problem. It will not be solved simply by unifying Viet Nam under one government, even if that government is competent. In fact, the difficulty is social rather than political. Put the traditional form of administration back in operation, as if exactly nothing had happened; suppose even—and this is a very optimistic supposition—that the war could be eliminated. Taxes would return. And where would one begin to look for a remedy for the lack of moral balance in the country? A better way of preparing a country for anarchy could not be found. It is a venture without an end. It would finish by creating a resistance, if one did not exist already.

Nothing is morally viable that does not start by giving back to the Vietnamese the conviction that they are living in *natural* groups—and yet, not the old ones, for nature has skipped a stage.

Except for the family, the traditional unities have been undone by the social and economic imbalance of the villages and the promiscuity of the cities. The old economy is gone beyond return. With usurers growing fat upon the land, accumulating urban fortunes and large landholdings, the dispossessed peasantry begins to lapse into a proletariat.

Capital must therefore be directed toward a technical and financial plan to equip the country to realize as much as she can from her own resources, if only for the educational value of such a plan. The villages will have to be re-established in natural groups, with a stable economy suitable to their introduction to the modern monetary system, in such a way that taxes will not make for dissolution. A program of cooperatives for consumers and producers should accomplish that. The best authorities agree that Viet Nam's history indicates such a course for her future development.

Such seem to me to be the real and constant elements which lie behind the moral instability and collective discord of the Vietnamese that observers on our side of the conflict think they see. Part, at least, of the solution must be sought in this quarter.

Many of the contributions of the Western world to Viet Nam will doubtless have to be kept by any modern Vietnamese state, but in a naturalized form. It will be far from easy to give back to the people of Viet Nam a conviction that they are living in natural groups viable in peace and order, without which nothing lasts. That much of the Confucian teaching is still applicable. But if such an order must be guaranteed, there arises the question, What does the West offer to replace the ritualistic state? That state assured unity and order in the world by a harmony between human institutions and the laws of nature, and the learning of China sustained that tranquillity. But, as the poet asked, where are the snows of yesteryear?

Those who now go to Viet Nam should appreciate the doubts that now assail the Vietnamese, less for themselves than for what, as a nation, is at stake for them. From the depths of their historical experience, they have drawn the conviction that peace on earth is the condition of all success, of every efficacious organization among individual nations.

Hard hit by the cosmic disorder of the age, they certainly have profound reasons for turning against the two nations of which they expect the most, France and the United States, and for holding these two countries responsible for the external situation which seems to paralyze them. But it should be understood that they do not specifically blame us; what they blame is the whole of occidental civilization (Communism included), and the worldwide split that has taken place. Occidental civilization is in danger of becoming for them the substitute for their traditional concept of a "denatured nature."

The Vietnamese were accustomed to place their culture and their national destiny in a unity of civilization. Nothing less will reassure them. It should not be forgotten that they still know little about the world beyond their own borders; consequently, at the same time that we are wondering about what kind of people they are, they are wondering about what kind of people we are. To tell them that heaven helps those who help themselves may not be quite to the point, for the solution to the present situation does not lie entirely with the Vietnamese.

2.

The Sources of the Vietnamese Political Tradition

The principal problems of Viet Nam—Communism or republican government, the program and future of political parties, armed resistance or cooperation for social reconstruction, agrarian reform and industrialization—cannot be seen clearly unless they are viewed from the perspective of the village community. From the very beginning of its history the authentic life of the country has been that of its villages. Despite the events of many centuries this is still essentially true.

However, the representatives of France tended to think of Viet Nam in terms of urban centers. This was natural because these cities, as areas of modern development, were French creations. But this view had significant consequences when France reoccupied Viet Nam in the autumn of 1945, after the Japanese capitulation ended World War II. A substantial portion of the Vietnamese who were becoming progressively more urbanized retreated from the cities and went back to the countryside and their ancestral customs which they had so recently abandoned. They settled down to a vegetative but enduring existence in their villages amidst the traditional tableau of rice fields, one next to another as far as the eye could see. This retreat to the countryside was a protest against the French reoccupation. It was a search for a basis from which to resist the restoration of the prewar status through a protracted struggle.

Once Hanoi and its suburbs were recaptured and cleared of the Viet Minh in early 1947, a French military offensive was launched during the autumn of that year against resistance bases in the mountains of Tonkin (northern Viet Nam). This operation, executed by paratroopers and riverborne commandos, proved definitely that the French armed forces were able to penetrate into any of the areas held by their adversaries. Except for short periods of inferiority in certain locations—due sometimes to a shortage of manpower, sometimes to the disposition of troops or to plans that were badly adapted to local conditions—this advantage was maintained. However, it did not bring about the political solution that the French general staff foresaw in 1947 as resulting from a campaign of local raids. Even though these operations were expanded they did not bring the French closer to their objective of an effective pacification of the rural areas. Subsequently, it was decided to replace the French Expeditionary Force with a Vietnamese national army, a force that had to be created from nothing. It was believed that a Vietnamese army could bring about the pacification that had continually eluded the French. But this was not a panacea either.

Although French forces proved capable of going anywhere in Viet Nam, they were rarely able to stabilize their conquests, except in certain urban areas. This fact was serious from a political standpoint not only for reasons of "face" but also because French occupation revealed their own local partisans while subsequent evacuation exposed them to destruction by the Viet Minh. This sequence of events showed that French occupation had been merely superficial. Despite undeniable French control in certain areas, the Viet Minh were able to reintroduce themselves clandestinely. They were able to make levies on the harvests and to collect taxes. French authority functioned in the daytime but the night belonged to the Viet Minh. This unceasing deterioration of everything that the French were attempting to rebuild, both materially and morally, gradually led them to an important change in policy. During the period 1946–1947, it is possible to follow this reorientation month by month in official declarations and in the commentaries of the French moderate press. No longer was France thinking in terms of a restoration of a colonial Indochina. Rather it became necessary to "liberate" Viet Nam from French sovereignty and to establish a national government, under the leadership of Emperor Bao Dai, that would oppose the Viet Minh.

The Political Power of Vietnamese Peasants

What did the scattered adversaries of the French have in hand against them that had caused a change in their policy? What was there in the Viet Nam of the rice fields that would not be subdued even though it was cut off from all administrative and industrial centralization? To answer these questions one must play a game. It must be set up on a chessboard—an expression which in this particular case is an apt description of the compartmented network of rice fields in the countryside. At the very foundation of Vietnamese society the rice fields have throughout history supplied this society with a reason for being. The fields have provided the basis for a stable social structure, a discipline for work, and a rhythm of communal celebrations—in short, a contract between the society itself, the soil, and the sky.

Within this limited framework adapted to their dispositions the Vietnamese found their style for living despite material privations. The French did their best to respect this traditional milieu while at the same time exposing it to ideas of a better way of life. Although the Vietnamese accepted the French into their countryside of traditional structures they were unable to alter the pattern of their life in the direction of French ideas. Since the elements of French civilization and its perspectives on political life are chiefly urban, they gave a very faint idea of the inner cohesion of a life close to the soil. During the ages this life has seemed changeless. Indeed, it has repeated itself from generation to generation. The Chinese conquests of Viet Nam, so socially and culturally effective, were merely secular episodes from the political point of view.

In Viet Nam millions of men cling to the surface of the flat and irrigable land. There swarm the villages—7,000 of them in the Red River Delta alone, where more than 7,000,000 inhabitants are crammed into 15,000 square kilometers. The village as a unit is the prime element in the human landscape. In fact, it fashioned that landscape and made the territory of Viet Nam what it is: a repetition of villages extending to its boundaries. Any action taken in the interior of this country will therefore imply the economic, social, and political re-equipment of these village settlements.

The harmony between the Vietnamese—who entered history in 208 B.C. somewhere around the southern edge of China—and their environmental conditions has proved to be so deep that no race has been able to resist their advance, nor has any force subsequently managed to wrench them from the land. The historic southward advance of the Vietnamese from the Red River Delta was facilitated by military operations. But it was consolidated by the peasantry, who extended their network of villages and destroyed all the vestiges of the defeated Kingdom of Champa, which lay in the path of the southern movement. In the eighteenth century a large part of Cochin China had been similarly taken away from the Cambodians, who were driven farther and farther back toward the west. Had the French not arrived, the remaining portion of Cambodia would have been the reward to a victor in a war between Viet Nam and Thailand. Vietnamese history thus poured down through Indochina like a flood sweeping away the other peoples wherever they inhabited flat land on which there were rice fields or which was favorable to the development of rice fields.

A further and conclusive proof of the harmony between the Vietnamese and flat lands suitable for rice cultivation is the fact that their expansion stopped at the foothills of the highlands. With the exception of certain political or military outposts, such as Cao Bang on the China border or the Pleiku enclave on the central plateau, the Vietnamese have not inhabited the mountain highlands of Viet Nam. In the relatively recent period during which France became associated with their history, the Vietnamese—having already moved from Tonkin all the way to the Gulf of Siam, a distance of nearly 1,200 miles—have made almost no inroads into the territory of the central plateau, the home of the *montagnards*. Their settlements have always been compressed between the mountains and the sea on a strip 600 miles long and in places only a few miles wide. Hemmed in at the west by the edge of these forest-clad slopes with their deadly endemic malaria, the Vietnamese gradually achieved their demographic equilibrium in the plains by means of irrigated rice cultivation.

In this open landscape dotted with villages the Vietnamese developed their way of life. According to Pierre Gourou[1] it was in these lowland plains that man found the development best suited to the circumstances of soil and climate on the level of a society of artisans in a tropical zone. Consequently, one can see that Vietnamese expansion represented a historical continuity. Everywhere that rice can be cultivated under water these Vietnamese agricultural communities have spread almost spontaneously. Although beaten militarily several times in history by the Chams, who lay in the path of their southward expansion, the Vietnamese not only defeated these rivals in the long run but also uprooted them. Somewhat like Islam, although with perhaps less ethical tolerance, the Vietnamese brought a complete life rather than a separate economy, faith, and system of law. The Vietnamese fashioned the country in their own image. Wherever that style of life succeeded the Vietnamese settled in, and experience has proved that they are there to stay.

A well-known hypothesis of Pierre Gourou's is that in a tropical country the cultivation of rice in flooded fields is what alone gives rise to the development of an advanced civilization, while at the same time limiting it. Vietnamese expansion corresponds to this historical point of view. Yet to explain its success in that way it is necessary to examine closely the social structure of the Vietnamese, because the Chams and the Cambodians were also acquainted with that method of growing rice. In fact the Vietnamese when they conquered the Chams did not restore all of their skillful irrigation systems. Historically it seems that the practical superiority of rural Vietnamese society is due to its harmony with the Chinese social system. Moreover, the weakness of the

1. Pierre Gourou is the author of *Les Paysans du delta Tonkinois: Etude de geographie humaine* (Paris, 1936; trans. by Richard R. Miller, *The Peasants of the Tonkin Delta: A Study of Human Geography* [New Haven: Human Relations Area Files, Inc., 1955]), 2 vols.; *L'Utilisation du sol en Indochine Francaise* (Paris, 1936); *L'Asie* (Paris, 1953); and *The Tropical Lands* (London, 1953).

adversaries of the Vietnamese can be attributed to their identification with the social principles and traditions of India.

The Vietnamese Model of China's Social System

What is the essence of Vietnamese culture? It would appear to have borrowed from its northern neighbor the strength to conquer its southern adversaries. But where did it derive the strength to resist the model it was patterned on and to throw off political domination after centuries of subjection? From the very beginning of Viet Nam the key answer to her historic problems would seem to be found in precisely that spirit of resistance. In a paradoxical way this spirit combines amazing powers of assimilation with a national invincibility that is proof against defeats, divisions, and conquests. More than a thousand years of annexation to China, from the second century B.C. to the tenth century A.D., far from having worn down that invincibility, seems instead to have strengthened it.

It is in Chinese annals that Viet Nam emerges from legend and enters history. During the first and second centuries B.C. she appears as a conquered province. The parceling out of the land, the source of local civilization, had obviously been handled by the colonists and the Chinese civil servants. Subsequently, the state, the official society, laws, army, letters, and the arts were gradually formed in Chinese fashion. Confucius was universally accepted in Viet Nam as in China and altars to him flourished even in the villages. But the basic structure, closely related to the rice fields, was modest. Needless to say, Viet Nam was never on the scale of that world in itself, China.

"In the first year of the *t'iao-lu* reign (A.D. 679)," reads a Chinese text translated by an eminent specialist on Viet Nam, Emile Gaspardone, a demanding and reliable scholar,

> Kao tsung of the T'ang dynasty transformed that region into a general protectorate of Annam. Actually the settlements were rustic and wretched, small walls and straw huts that other people would never have lived in. Then Li Cong Uan, gradually imitating China, estab-

lished commanderies and subprefectures. Yet the whole country was hardly more than a Chinese province. A secondary prefecture consisted of a little over ten villages a subprefecture in one or two villages. The Chinese who had just arrived in the country would laugh secretly at this each time.

Traditional Vietnamese scholars adopted the notion that this process was characteristic of the way in which the country assimilated classical Chinese culture. But such an attitude, followed literally, would be an overstatement. Indeed, once the swampy forests of the Red River Delta were cleared and dried, when the country was transformed into rice fields and a government established, what had emerged was in no way a new Chinese province but rather a nation with an unyielding sense of its own identity. In Kwangtung, Kwangsi, and Yunnan, Chinese civilization created China out of disparate ethnic elements. To the south of these provinces, in an area under the same Chinese cultural influence, it was, on the contrary, Viet Nam that was created. For more than 2,000 years the Vietnamese carried on an inner resistance in an unequal struggle against Chinese culture. From the very beginning and from the very depths of themselves they must have escaped from the official formalism that had become characteristic of Chinese civilization.

The Village Foundation of Vietnamese Society

It would seem that from the outset of the agricultural organization of the country, the Vietnamese village by its very rusticity had been an inviolable sanctuary for the nation. It was not that each village was capable of resisting individually. But these villages were found everywhere. They were not concentrated in any one place so that the adversary might have seized them as one lays hold of a capital, overthrows a dynasty, or subjugates a court. How wrong the Chinese were to laugh secretly at such humble institutions, for these institutions never yielded to them. Viet Nam is above all a way of being and living whose expression and means of expansion are the village. The profusion of villages and the uniform shapes of its rice fields have given definition to the land wherever it has been taken over from savage nature or from other peoples. This is the perspective from which the secret and opaque, although human, character of the nation can best be seen.

From another perspective high in the air, these rural settlements between their tall hedges give the impression of being baskets. Inside one can see low gray or brown roofs amidst a tangle of small gardens, lanes, and blind alleys arranged like the "teeth of a comb," to use a picturesque local expression. It is a space which is to a high degree cramped and divided. From the ground, on the contrary, everything changes and nothing looks as it has just been described. The social space and its divisions have vanished behind a kind of fleeting perspective which is impossible to penetrate. The bamboo hedges rise straight up around the village like rocks. The villages slide one behind another in the landscape as the passer-by follows the unavoidable windings of the causeway that forms a path. These anonymous masses of bamboo hedge make up a moving and continuous horizon which always encircles the spectacle of the rice fields and the manifold work it implies. Thus it is man who himself makes his own horizon behind which his real life may be hidden. After going mile after mile in the Vietnamese countryside one has the impression of having stood still.

In a country politically fashioned, as this one has been throughout the centuries, by conquest, resistance, conspiracy, rebellion, and dissension, any clandestine activity is subject to special rules laid down by the particular social and physical milieu. Here again we must enter into another world, leaving aside what we know is done in our own. In these plains of irrigated rice there are ordinarily no natural sanctuaries in which one may hide: no woods, no marshlands or moors. If man wants to take cover and disappear he can only do so behind man. Consequently, this type of disappearance is a solution only for those people native to the region. But with that reservation the populous masses are an effective shelter against any adversary of a different language, or more especially, of a different skin.

When a man creeps in among his own people, how can he be

found? In the last analysis it is the villages that have the answer. As a result, they are always on guard and suspicious about everything that comes from the outside. They keep any stranger at a distance even if he is of the same race. Nor do they welcome any passing guest until they are sure of his identity and his intentions—although they are never too quick to believe in either. A stranger must not be in a hurry to explain. If the truth is reassuring he must let them discover it themselves. They have their methods acquired by varied experience over the centuries. A guest who is accepted feels altogether at home, and the hospitality he finds in the Vietnamese village is not an empty word. If he has met with approval as regards rules and conventions he, too, is sheltered by the hedge. Paul Mus knew this from personal experience.

The villages, then, are what constitute Viet Nam, and only through them does one in crucial times learn to know the country and its national spirit. Pierre Gourou has strikingly expressed these values that are so fundamental to the country:

> At the same time as being a protection against outside dangers, the hedge is a kind of sacred boundary of the village community, the sign of its individuality and its independence. When in times of dissension a village has been a party to the agitation or has given asylum to rebels, the first punishment inflicted upon it is that of forcing it to cut its bamboo hedge. This is a serious blow to its pride, a stamp of dishonor. The village feels as uncomfortable as a human being would were he undressed and marooned in the middle of a fully dressed crowd.

This image is eminently fitting. It enables us to grasp the society made up of adjacent villages formed among themselves, like actual persons, through their community of feelings and conventions. Indeed, Viet Nam owes its success throughout its history to the cohesion and enterprise of those institutions. They even resisted China while absorbing her culture.

There we have the traditional framework. But how does it adapt to the drama being played out today?

Western observers are too apt to attribute a uniformly conservative spirit to the villages. This tends to be done because the villages constitute the static mass of the people. The traditional mentality of the villages is readily contrasted with the aspirations of the "intellectuals," those active, impatient, but not very numerous city people who have been educated through their relations with France and according to French patterns. Is this contrast, which was surely true in the first decade of this century, still of any value? No. And an unprejudiced glance at the situation in the early 1950's would support this opinion. Across from the French defensive perimeter the "dissident" zone had a reputation for "revolutionary" obedience. Now this zone was essentially made up of a network of villages which had gone over to the armed resistance or at least were helping to feed the resistance. The French, on the other hand, were more successful in holding the cities. There the conservative elements united with the French side.

Has progressivism changed partners and have these two aspects in the country changed sides? No, but there has been a semantic change. The fact of this semantic change had to be acknowledged when the French realized the political contrast between the checkered countryside and the cities scattered here and there. The real situation could no longer be suitably described in abstract political terms, such as progressivism and conservatism, which were perhaps still valid at the time of our elders. In all fairness, let us first put aside the easy formula according to which we would be dealing with an apathetic peasantry. In this archaic view the peasants are concerned solely with their daily bowl of rice and are terrorized by a handful of agitators. The substance of current difficulties comes perhaps from that initial error of interpretation.

The fact that France made this error shows that she was not sensitive to the national resurgence in Viet Nam during the Japanese occupation. After the Japanese capitulation, in the midst of the Franco-Vietnamese war, Paul Mus covered over a hundred miles in Tonkin on foot, going into the combat zone and finally through the Vietnamese lines in search of Ho Chi Minh. There he saw people who had found an equilibrium. They were on guard in outposts only six miles from Hanoi, for the French zone of occupation was limited to that, and at work everywhere else. Since then this resistance has not been broken down in any lasting way by either French or American political action or repeated military operations.

This resistance testified to national cohesion. Cut back and reduced to its network of villages, Viet Nam held fast more easily than other nations would have done. The reason for this resilience was her basic historical structure. This self-withdrawal was signified by the phenomenon that everywhere the people tore down brick houses, especially the multistoried ones in urban centers, ostensibly because they might be used as blockhouses for French paratroopers. The resistance seemed to feel at home under a "straw hut." And it is here that France, and now America, had to seek it out and seek to understand it no matter whether one wished to win it back, disarm it, or try to conquer it.

3.

The Mandate of Heaven: Politics as Seen from the Vietnamese Village

Sheltered behind ponds and impenetrable bamboo hedges, which rise, like veritable brown and green cliffs, straight up in the rice fields, the villages of Viet Nam used to be self-governing, with a deep-rooted autonomy guaranteed by statutes. According to an old Vietnamese proverb, "the law of the Emperor yields to the custom of the village." But a more substantial guarantee of village autonomy than this proverb was the lack of a compulsory registration of births and deaths by the central administration of the traditional state. When it was necessary to determine the collective obligations of each village in paying taxes, raising *corvées,* or supplying a contingent of soldiers for the national army, the state had to depend on inadequate village registers. These registers were manifestly incomplete, and although they were supposedly rectified every five years, they remained for the central authorities a deceptive source of information on village population. Consequently, they were an effective check on the power of the central administration over village affairs.

A council of notables was jointly responsible for the collective obligations of the village. It was recruited from the small oligarchy of the village and had associated with it as advisers a number of literati and retired civil servants. Once collective obligations were fulfilled, the council of notables had nothing else to account for to the central administration but criminal matters. Its functions included the selection of village officials as well as overseeing the routine of village administration. Overall, the temporal relations with the state were never more than statistical, whereas its dealings with the people under its jurisdiction were, on the contrary, personal and direct. The council knew the names of all the inhabitants of the village and kept track of their affairs, but it never imparted those names. Therefore, the state's power extended only to the imposition of a tax or other obligation on the village as a whole; it did not deal with the individual, the *dân,* except when criminal charges were involved. And despite the numerous changes in ruling dynasties this autonomy of the village was maintained, without any great change, until the beginning of the twentieth century.

It has now become usual to speak of a constant, though veiled, conflict between the two extreme elements of traditional Vietnamese politics: on the one hand the Emperor, the court, and the mandarin system of bureaucratic administration; on the other, those village authorities fortified morally and even physically within the enclosure of their villages. However, upon more careful consideration, one gets the impression of a skillful division of labor. The state—from the military, judicial, and religious point of view—was centralized and authoritarian. No village could have defied it with impunity. But because of the distribution of administrative duties between it and the villages, especially in economic matters, the state weighed lightly. All dealings and services of a public nature had been decentralized to the highest degree and put into the hands of the village and district authorities. There was also decentralization with regard to the actual remuneration of the administrative bodies, because they were paid mostly in kind—that is to say, in rice—by the villagers themselves. Taken as a whole this system resulted in the state's having a very small monetary budget.

Having come up against this centuries-old tradition, France allowed herself to be led in turn by two sometimes contradictory approaches: a desire to modernize and to promote cultural assimilation with the West, primarily due to pressure from home; and locally, a certain degree of mistrust among Vietnamese conservatives about the effects of a precipitous evolution toward modernity. The colonial experts had plenty of arguments against the conservatives, but they nevertheless chose to put their confidence in traditional Vietnamese institutions. In the last fifty years of French rule the modernist tendency won out on the whole, but not without a few serious defeats and some remorse. This trend was manifested in three series of acts:

1. The creation of a proper system of registering births and deaths in the villages. This tended to straighten out the tax lists.
2. Increased control over the council of notables by French administrators with regard to organizing the village budget and putting it into effect.
3. An attempt to replace cooptation with election as a means of recruiting the council of notables.

The intention of these "reforms" was to bring Vietnamese institutions into line with the communal organization of France. Obviously, such innovations were bound to cause deep disturbances in local life.

The Effect of Colonial "Reforms"

The traditional system had been sustained for centuries by resources which were hidden from the central authorities by the absence of a responsible procedure for registering village population. The number of persons registered determined the sum total of impositions—taxes and *corvées*—that the village owed to the state. But the actual number of villagers, diligently concealed from the central authorities, was ordinarily much higher than that registered. This difference between the tax to be paid collectively by the village and the total of what was actually taxable produced a kind of parafiscal reserve that remained at the disposal of the village authorities and was used for village welfare and emergencies. As the keeping of the registry became more reliable through French regulation, this exploitable margin was naturally curtailed. The colonial administration's control managed to become stronger and to cut down, or at least make difficult, the exploitation of the village fiscal reserves by the local councils.

The third series of measures mentioned above were political in nature. They were supposed to prompt the taxpayers to keep a sharper eye on communal affairs because they had become electors. In 1921 in Tonkin the French paved the way for an evolution in that direction. In so doing the French administration anticipated that the mass election of former notables would occur because of their knowledge of local interests, as well as their traditional prestige and experience. This continuity was expected to facilitate the change to the new system; but such was not the case.

The election results were confusing and disappointing. In some villages certain French-educated Vietnamese might have been tempted to run for seats in the new councils, but ordinarily such men did not carry much weight in local affairs. Their qualifications provoked more jealousy or mistrust than emulation. The new order they represented broke too abruptly with the recognized elements of the society. The village showed no willingness to introduce new values, along with the men who stood for them, into its own affairs. As for the notables, who were the customary leaders of the rural population, they had too much to lose financially by the change. They therefore withdrew from participation and saw to it that rather unrepresentative men were elected. Without coming forward themselves, the notables maneuvered other men into position and then conducted a veiled opposition to all the measures recommended by the colonial administration.

Thus it would seem that French attempts at modernization on the village level were a failure. Slowly, it became clear that these changes were not at all welcome in the countryside, and with understandable defensiveness, Frenchmen considered this utter lack of enthusiasm for these innovations a result of Viet Nam's political and civic immaturity. Others saw it as proof of a vitality generated by traditional values and directed against the intemperate modernism of the French. Despite this disagreement over the reasons for the unpopularity of the councils there was no dispute about their effectiveness. Elected councils, instituted in Tonkin in 1921, were ultimately abolished by an imperial decree issued by Bao Dai in 1941, which restored former prerogatives and powers to the traditional councils of notables. But in 1945 these customary village councils which had been so recently re-established were swept away in many parts of Viet Nam along with the traditional monarchy following the advent of the revolutionary regime. The Communist-led Democratic Republic of Viet Nam then worked to rebuild the peasant society around councils of a different nature whose political foundations broke with the past. In many places it was a violent break. Yet there are "experts" on Vietnamese society who judge that all it would take to bring back peace to that shattered country is the gradual re-establishment of the customary network of village councils together with their traditional social values.

There lies the whole Viet Nam problem, no longer theoretical, but on the level of actual institutions.

When the colonial regime was destroyed by the Japanese occupation of Indochina and the armed indigenous resistance in 1945, a decision had to be made by the revolutionaries on the future status of the village councils. The resulting choice was to eliminate them, and this meant that the councils of notables were dispersed and occasionally decimated in areas where the Viet Minh had strength. This measure was *the* major act in the domestic history of the Democratic Republic of Viet Nam for it was doubtless the one that most determined its future. The decision would appear to have been provoked by two considerations. First, a broad and systematic national policy found expression in the immediate replacement of the customary councils by a new type of village committee. Second, in support of these new committees there was a regrouping of Vietnamese village society in a pattern that was radically different from its traditional structure. There were worker and peasant unions as well as committees made up of women, the aged, and even children, plus groups of tradesmen, former military men, and others with a differentiated social status.

The Mandate of Heaven and the Concept of Revolution

This social and political revolution was not merely imposed from the top down but had local antecedents that gave it real roots in the countryside. For instance, during the last decades of the colonial period the French had caused the villages to consider themselves opponents to the traditional monarchy France was "protecting." In the local way of looking at things, the villages were credited with having a "virtue"—that is, a political and social system—which was antagonistic to the monarchy in power, and within this Confucian tradition, which was still deeply rooted in the countryside, there was no room for a compromise. Either there was close identification or antagonism. Moreover, by regarding history as involving a complete change, this tradition also includes a conception of revolution that might be called cosmic or climactic; in fact, it is invariably expressed as such in Chinese texts. According to them, at critical moments institutions, doctrines, and the men in power change entirely, as a unity, just as one season replaces another.

The whole apparatus of repression such as it was, was organized in Viet Nam in the name of the traditional monarchy, but in fact carried out by the French colonial authorities, prepared the minds of the people for precisely such ideas. Consequently, from the very moment in 1945 that the supporters of the revolutionary party changed over from the position of dissenters to a mastery of the situation, they were expected to eliminate all the elements of the former system; compromises were not anticipated. Although the doctrine of the Viet Minh was not known in detail, it hardly mattered, since the doctrine had only to make a general impression on the minds of the people, who could then take a position for or against it. Traditionally it was quite characteristic of Vietnamese village politics that the up-and-coming clique easily found partisans apart from any ideological preferences, because the closed milieu of the village, within which there are veiled and endlessly reiterated conflicts, yielded adherents to a new regime from among the usual adversaries of the notables. Moreover, the notables are normally shaken by the fall of the old order, and as for the masses, they go along with the new order if it lasts.

Behind the ease of accepting such a new regime may be seen the wisdom of a people who through experience have learned that changes in government are above all formal and not substantive. But together with such considerations of form, which are so important in East Asia, there are some moral notions which must not be underestimated. Every system has its flaws and all fall into abuse; yet a natural tendency of people identified with Chinese civilization is to put up with abuses in normal times for lack of being able to do anything about them. Despite their desires for an end of abuses the desire for stability has been uppermost in their minds; consequently, they sought a political system capable of sustaining itself, a condition which they called the "virtue" of the dynasty.

But the behavior of those same very docile masses is something else indeed when a revolution is proclaimed, and the West is forever surprised by it. The moment a "virtue" (in the West one would say a political system) appears to be worn out and another is in view ready to take the place of the old, the previous abuses —which had been put up with until then—are seen in a new light. Then, and only then, must they be remedied with the help of a new principle. Extreme patience is thus replaced by intolerance. First the people tolerate everything. Then they refuse to put up with anything. In other words, the former values don't count any more.

This is how the civic morality of East Asia, which has often been accused of being more lax than that of the West regarding the mistakes of the powers that be, their demands, the misappropriation of funds, etc., suddenly become intransigent. This is not opportunism but rather another intellectual rhythm, one different from that of the West. It has nothing whatever to do with political pretexts. Involved here are moral values comparable to the highest of those in the West, but they are put into practice only when the circumstances are clearly appropriate. Such behavior derives from a centuries-old wisdom leading to civic reactions that are in no way similar to ours. Instead of going along at a moderate but continuous and slowly effective pace, the Sino-Vietnamese moral life jumps, spasmodically, from crisis to crisis far more than does that of the West.

When a crisis comes, the minds of the people suddenly become susceptible to moral values and more attentive to the mistakes that have been made. They judge these errors to have been at the roots of the revolution, and, therefore, the behavior of the protagonists has a determining influence on events. It is not by accident that East Asia prefers to use the word "virtue" for what the West would call a "system." Also, East Asia is more easily resigned than is the West to a lack of daily bursts of morality from an established regime. On the other hand, the usual reaction of the people, especially the masses, to a change in regime is to come up with a prognosis and to choose accordingly by evaluating the opposing virtues or what would appear as such. Have we probed deeply enough into this exceptional mentality and understood from the very depths of the Vietnamese countryside the effect it has and the practical demands it makes? A few more illustrations will help us toward that understanding.

The Traditional Symbols of Vietnamese Politics

In normal times there is a sure but limited propaganda value in appealing to peasant villagers with symbols of flaunted poverty and an ascetic way of life. This kind of virtue, which the popular soul likens to the cycle of fire, penitence, and purification, may then yield to the promises of another system reflecting abundance. Although such symbols may seem strange, they are direct and vital means of communication to a village world. For everyone in Viet Nam, and especially the propertied and ruling classes, the shape of power has a symbolic nature. The Chinese character *yuan,* which means "round" and evokes the fullness of a circle, was the generic term used to designate respectable things, especially the authority of the mandarins. During the time of revolution, other, opposing symbols are employed by the competitors for power. Such imagery is not devoid of hidden political significance. Indeed, the East Asian mind has proved to be so deeply permeated by it that no action there would go very far were it not to be taken into account.

As an attempt in this direction the French in their propaganda made use of an oversimple and suggestive image that reduced social conflicts to "the struggle of the thin against the fat." Asia, with its political antitheses, acknowledges a duality of the same kind but one that is much more profound. In the adaptation of Asia to the modern elements of international politics it is necessary to elucidate these traditional ways of seeing and speaking. It is also important to realize that the civic and political education of the Vietnamese, although considered recent by Western standards, in fact has a background of one or two thousand years. This has included an understanding of seemingly abstract themes whose practical implications it would be very wrong to underestimate.

Even among a people for whom geomancy and astrology have great influence, the importance of geometrical symbols would not alone explain a choice between two political systems, or two "virtues." But the substance of beliefs, intuitions, and feelings that they convey proves to be of the greatest importance when the choice is being made. Many eddies in the consciousness of the people, which are indecipherable for Westerners—who then speak of betrayal or ingratitude—may be explained in this way.

The men who dominate politics in the villages and the countryside have never lacked the mental resources to follow in a penetrating peasant fashion the evolution of a political situation. Public life exists behind the screen of bamboo hedges and has a rhythm of its own. It can be seen from what has been said above how and within what limits political success proves to be anticipated. It can also be seen why people spontaneously expect that a party that seizes power in the name of a radically new principle of the state will not come to terms with anything that has preceded it. The established values are overthrown and obliterated; the state changes not only in appearance but also in essence.

The only revolutions that Vietnamese political wisdom considers authentic are those that effect complete change. The main proof of a party's right to power is a program that provides new solutions for everything, and in East Asia this conception has forever been familiar to the simplest countryman. But is he prepared to hear the current language of the social and political revolution that is spreading in his direction from its center in northeastern Europe, which says, "The very foundation of the world is going to change. . . ." In answering this, one must remember that there is a very important difference in the Asian concept of revolution; Asians do not believe that the struggle will have an ultimate end. The Asian mind believes only in mutations within precise limits against a permanent background.

In 1945–46, the Vietnamese village notables bore the costs of one of these mutations. Although the events were often tragic and differed altogether from the normal course of peasant life, they were prompted by a spirit that is traditional in certain respects. Without even having to think about the coordination and organization established in this instance by an extremist party, the Viet Minh and its far-reaching revolutionary network, each peasant was historically prepared to understand the sudden turn of events and to accept it with a fatalistic air. The cruel fate of the local authorities who were answerable for the system that was being overthrown was tangible proof of what the revolutionaries presented as a "renovation of the state."

Because of his potential for such political sagacity, it is an odd mistake to believe that the Vietnamese common man is concerned with nothing but his bowl of rice. Of course, it is one of his main preoccupations. But he has definite ideas about who can assure him of it or take it away from him, and they go a long way. For centuries, even in the poorest villages, there were a few local literati who progressively familiarized the national consciousness with the principles of Chinese political thought. Though this thought is disconcerting to Westerners in its expressions and images, it is well adapted to the village domain. Therefore, the great historic events do not leave the people indifferent, especially when they are directly concerned and will be affected by them even in their rural retreats. An unerring instinct assures them that in crucial times their own reaction is what in the last resort determines the fate of the nation. They have learned this principle from the disciples of Confucius and Mencius. Of course, the *dân* does not build, but he chooses between systems and thus with his collective strength decides between the "virtues" that come into conflict before him and about him. It is up to him through that

choice to sanction the system, or "virtue," that is in hamony with
fate; Westerners have a suitable expression for this choice: the
historical moment. In the eyes of the Vietnamese such moments
are marked by the irresistible force with which events are pre-
cipitated.

The Sign of an Authentic Revolution

To appear before the people, the supreme judge, with any
chance of success as a messenger of fate, a revolutionary party
must show them all the signs of its mission. In this case the people
expect the sign of signs: the ease and fluidity of success. The revolutionary party must succeed in everything as if miraculously. The
military and financial means are in the popular opinion, if not in
fact, secondary considerations and will of their own accord put
themselves in the hands of the party that has received the "mandate of heaven." In this light it is profitable to consider the as-
tounding scenario presented by the advent of the Democratic
Republic of Viet Nam at Hanoi in August, 1945, and the effect it
must have had on the Vietnamese masses.

This bid for revolutionary power occurred amidst a whirlpool
that swept everything away—the Japanese occupation forces, foreigners of all kinds, and the national dynasty. Almost without
firing a shot, yesterday's outlaws became on the international
scene the leaders of the country and proclaimed themselves
heaven-sent in the most classical of traditions. Their success was
not regarded as being helped along by the absence of reaction
from the Japanese occupation forces. Therefore, the state of mind,
so to speak, of all Viet Nam could not fail to transmit the great
jolt all the way to the farthest villages. Everything was possible,
indeed inevitable, in the countryside the minute heaven's decision
was manifested in such an unimpeachable way in the capital.

In these revolutionary circumstances it is useful to reflect on
the importance of the figurehead who is representative of the
revolutionary party. Since everything is interrelated and everything
is the sign of heaven's choice, there is no better political resource
than judging by the character of the man what he will bring with

him. The Chinese tradition carried this sense of wholeness to such an extreme that on the advent of a new dynasty there were extensive changes. Customs, clothing, and certain written words were adjusted according to the individual traits of the new Emperor. For example, the road measurements marked by milestones were recalculated by adjusting the cubit to the actual measure of the Emperor's forearm.

Everything considered, the international press and world opinion was not wrong when they tried to schematize the Vietnamese conflict by opposing two characters, each of which is representative of opposing political principles. On the other side there was the former outlaw, Nguyen the Patriot—a translation of Ho Chi Minh's early alias, which conveys the sentimental flavor it has in the Vietnamese language—who has become President of a government. Across from him there was the head of the vestigial Nguyen dynasty, Emperor Bao Dai, who was designated by prevailing circumstances as the only other partner in this game of fate. But if we mix Western ideas with the game these antagonists are playing, its significance will be missed. The Western tendency is to evaluate each of the two players in terms of what he really represents: appraisals are made of his strength and backing. The number of his respective supporters, declared and undeclared, are calculated along with the number of advocates of a wait-and-see policy on either side. Perhaps the Vietnamese intellectuals and politicians who were schooled in the French tradition sometimes imitate the French in making such a calculation. Doubtless that is why they make the same mistakes as the French.

The people themselves don't appear to take such a view of things. In fact it is their ignorance of the calculable elements and their logical lack of interest in them that has prompted so many good "colonial" experts to deny the people any political activity or maturity. But in the last analysis their reserve and their instinctive reactions have perhaps more significance than the critics would give them credit for. Instead of comparing total strength by adding up the men and the arms, which are all concrete elements, the Vietnamese peasant who has remained within the boundaries of his traditional horizon would be more apt to interrogate fate and the adaptation of men to that fate. He wonders whether such a leader, such a type of man of action, is in accordance with that indescribable something which has no name in our language but which in Vietnamese is called *Thiên minh*. A weak translation of those words would be "the will of heaven," or "the heavenly mandate."

The real factor in such powerful waves of opinion is that in critical times the Vietnamese people have, just as Westerners do, the deep and almost religious conviction of bearing within themselves the voice of heaven. At that particular moment the voice of heaven is their voice. Why should they make every effort to add up the partisans on either side in order to come to an individual opinion? When the time comes, the coalescence of mass support will bring an easy success to the party of heaven's choice. After the event this success proves that their choice was the right one.

It is never very easy to play with these latent forces of opinion, which, when they break loose in Asia, are irresistible. But how is it possible to avoid going off on the wrong track when pitting oneself against these forces without knowing about them? The Vietnamese people are not lost in the clouds even though they take their direction from them. After all, they would know how to count battalions and to judge the material elements of a situation. In fact, their natural tendency would be to magnify such calculations, but in their eyes these calculations are not enough. To feel really convinced they wait for events to take on a strong momentum consistent with their inner feelings and their expectations; only then are they persuaded that the greater force they were looking for has truly come into play. Of course, that force is linked to its material elements, but these elements are useful to it only as a sign of its presence—as a means of achieving its purpose.

This wisdom of the Vietnamese, in which they identify themselves with a winner, is a pragmatic wisdom common to all people. It does not spread but is transposed, from continent to continent, having each time a human substance and practical maxims of action that may be disconcerting. The coincidence of its formulas sheds light on the whole question of cross-cultural politics. In the West, for example, one speaks of "showing our strength to avoid using it." The only danger would be to believe that these words mean the same in Southeast Asia as they do in the West. Actually, in Southeast Asia they convey the substance of the Chinese tradition and a whole philosophy of the world, but in an important transposition. In their terms, might is never right, contrary to the aphorism of Western cynics. It is, however, far from denied or neglected; it is feared, dodged, shunned, used, but it is held in contempt. It must give one further sign: a specific indication of not having to be used. It then becomes not a positive, constructive fact but a sign. The only sign on which a government may establish itself in public opinion is the sign which is recognized as an edict, a mandate from heaven. In the Sino-Vietnamese tradition this divine superiority was called the government of open hands, or hands hanging open. It is the opposite, even to the image itself, of a certain Western *Faustrecht,* or mailed fist.

In order to understand the course of the Vietnamese revolution, the great omens that were evident in 1945 can never be emphasized enough. The swift rise to power of the Democratic Republic of Viet Nam was achieved by a small group of men who took advantage of these popular attitudes, attitudes which invested the group and its actual endeavors with a legitimacy that extended far beyond the region they controlled militarily. Let it not be forgotten that from the point of view of the common man in the rice field the abdication of Emperor Bao Dai in 1945 was an important symbolic event. This was especially true because he declared that he wanted to enter the ranks of this newly constituted people as a plain individual. What a mutation for Confucians to reflect upon! How easy for them to imagine that in these events was an expression of the power of the new system, a revolutionary "virtue" supported by a new world in conflict with the old order. This was a "virtue" that had been ripened in opposition and exile to bear fruit in this fateful hour.

To be sure, what followed after the first days of the revolution was not quite in line with what that brilliant beginning seemed to promise. The Viet Minh was not able to consolidate its power throughout Viet Nam even though the monarchy, historically linked to France as a protectorate, yielded without a struggle to the revolutionary government. In deferring to the revolutionaries the monarchy publicly claimed that its alliance with France had been the cause of its downfall, but this abdication was thought by the people to be a sign of heavenly decision, which would result in France being driven from Viet Nam. In a special sense this was a misleading sign based on the fact that the Allies had eliminated France from their councils, and without French participation it was decided by the Allies that Indochina would be occupied by Chinese troops to the north of the sixteenth parallel and by British forces to the south. The Allies' task was to accept the surrender of the Japanese forces in the territory, and there was no thought of using French forces for this mission. On land, on sea, and in the air the French flag seemed to have disappeared. From a local perspective the English and the Americans had apparently crossed France off the map of Asia as a colonial power.

4.

Revolution and the Politics of Modernization

The conservatism of the villages used to be contrasted with the new aspirations of those relatively few urban intellectuals whose attitudes were molded by contact with French culture. In the present situation, however, it is chiefly the conservative elements that seem to have congregated in the cities, while large areas of the countryside have resorted to armed resistance under leftist leadership. The explanation of this anomaly is not that the two groups have exchanged positions, but rather that formulas of a generation ago no longer apply.

It is essential to discard at once any notion that in Viet Nam the West is dealing with nothing more than a mass of apathetic peasants who have been terrorized by their leaders. When Paul Mus went in search of Ho Chi Minh in 1947 behind Communist lines, he found widespread evidence of an organized popular movement both at the front and in the rear.

On what ruins was this new order built? Many old institutions have certainly been destroyed, and in more than one instance, especially in the south, the notables who represented them have been executed by their own countrymen. What were the historical antecedents of these events, and to what extent was the sad fate of these notables due to their former activities? In waging an anti-revolutionary campaign in the Vietnamese countryside, the West has sometimes been tempted to employ the complex of communal

This chapter appeared in a slightly different version under the title, "The Role of the Village in Vietnamese Politics," in *Pacific Affairs*, Vol. XXII (September, 1949), pp. 265–72. It appears here by permission of the editor.

institutions for security purposes (including information, propaganda, and repression), but they could not do so without converting it into a political tool and thus warping it from its normal functions. In both the uprisings of 1930 and those of 1940–41 this complex was used for such purposes, a fact which may explain why, since 1945, when new leaders took over, the traditional institutions have been subverted by conditions utterly alien to the rhythm of village life.

The French are inclined to write history from official records, thus running the risk of attaching too much importance to official orders instead of investigating their actual results in the field. History thus conceived is really little more than a record of intentions. And, although French intentions in the matters under discussion have been expressed excellently, the concrete results are surely more significant. Why is it that none of their plans concerning rural organization, always so wisely motivated even though sometimes contradictory in effect, ever produced the expected results?

One explanation, accepted in certain of the conservative and traditionally anti-French Vietnamese circles on which French policy became dependent, interpreted French communal policy as a deliberate attempt to curb the councils of notables by bringing them ever more closely under French administrative control. If the French at first altered and then abolished the traditional status of the councils, their purpose, according to these critics, was to convert the councils into instruments of their own. If the French subsequently changed their tactics yet again and restored power to the councils, that was simply in order to secure an even firmer grip on them through a return to traditional forms, which the French recognized to be more effective. In any event, the French failure in this respect would be due to noncooperation on the part of the notables in the face of unreasonable demands.

At first sight this argument seems to contain a grain of truth. The French did indeed gain control of the councils of notables, and did burden them with evermounting responsibilities until they became accountable for a great variety of things: for tax collections and labor recruiting for different purposes; for prevention of damage to transportation and communications installations and equipment; for care of forestlands; for suppression of alcohol smuggling; and so forth.[1]

The Problems of Building a Modern State

Yet, for a clear view of the question, one should take into account the problems that confronted the French authorities. Some of their difficulties were involved in their colonial objectives; others were due to local conditions. The main problem still confronting Viet Nam today is basically one of transition—from a loosely knit, inexpensive, traditional state to a modern organization with a large budget. In the earlier form, inspired by Confucianism, centralization in religious and military matters was offset by decentralization in economic and social affairs. The king delivered judgments, bestowed titles, tried to expand his territory, and, most important, by means of unending ritual observances sought the favor of the gods on behalf of the people. For the rest, the life of the country was concentrated in the villages, and the costs of the central administration were accordingly slight.

The army comprised contingents provided and maintained by the villages, and public works were carried on by *corvées* recruited in similar fashion. Except for a few engaged in producing luxury items, no urban group of artisans was able to support itself on the low prices with which rural handicraftsmen, whose main source of livelihood remained the land, were satisfied—and this was one reason for the small number of cities. The busy rural marketplaces contributed little to the state revenues, which a century ago were estimated at only 3 million francs. Nor did the state provide any of the economic or other services essential to a modern society.

In order to survive, the country needed new and larger facilities —railways, highways, telecommunications, industries, financial

---

1. An extreme-leftist source has described the steep rise in local tax assessments in the following terms: "Between 1890 and 1896 direct taxes doubled. Between 1896 and 1898 they increased by one-half again. The villages had no alternative but to accept these increases because there was nobody to whom they could protest."

and commercial establishments, educational and public health equipment—as well as a fresh understanding of their uses. Clearly such needs exceeded by far the resources at the command of the Vietnamese government as long as its revenues depended on the traditional administrative structure. The new administrative system, the onus for whose unpopularity was borne mainly by French colonialism, was therefore not simply an outgrowth of a "colonial" outlook. Whatever the immediate goals of French policy in Viet Nam, the over-all shaping factor was the need to adapt the economy to modern requirements. And this was impossible unless the fabric of society was reshaped.

For example, when the French first installed a telegraph system in the country, the peasants were delighted: they speedily removed the overhead lines and put them to various uses in their homes. To stop this practice, the French made the village notables responsible for the protection of the telegraph lines—and also for the supervision of forestlands, highways, and waterworks as well as tax returns. In other words, as the demands of the new civilization increased, the obligations of the councils of notables became proportionately greater.

The drama peculiar to Viet Nam, as shaped by history and geography, is that once these needs had been calculated in accordance with the new ideas, it was necessary to meet them out of existing resources, the greater part of which were dependent on the old order. For the traditional world was not dead; it still held sway in the countryside, even though its scale of economic values was highly anachronistic. In 1939 the annual budget of a peasant family with eleven members was found to be 32 piastres—a sum indicative of a static economy. Of this total, direct taxes took 6 piastres, or 19 percent! Yet in certain areas it was customary to pay but one cent for a whole day's work. For a workman to receive one cent for a day's work and to have to pay about 6 piastres as an annual personal tax makes no sense whatsoever. The first figure reflects the monetary value of labor in the traditional society; the second expresses its value in a modern economy.

Such a state of affairs, in which the people's livelihood is calculated in terms of one world and their taxes in those of quite another, cannot endure. The Vietnamese peasant must therefore adapt himself to new circumstances: he must henceforth consider his personal budget in terms of monetary value rather than of immediate personal needs, and accustom himself to the concept of extrinsic value—a notion quite foreign to his traditional outlook. But it is quite clear that once he has learned to calculate his own economic capacity in such modern terms—and learn he must if the national exchequer is to meet its growing expenses—he will no longer be content with a nonindividualized status within a gregarious traditional community, governed by the council of notables. This is the price that must be paid if the country is to develop economically and to justify its claim to nationhood in the modern world.

In some respects French colonial administration provided the catalyst that hastened the advent of this necessary period of transition, and the two decades of war have deepened the social revolution and given it an air of paroxysmal violence. Basically, however, the present process of change stems from an economic revolution on a national, or even a world, rather than a colonial, level. A modern-style monetary tax, based on the regular registration of births and deaths, induces the taxpayers to consider their rights and duties, strips them of their cloak of communal anonymity, and converts them into individuals who must be reckoned with in social and political as well as in economic affairs. It is safe to predict that in Viet Nam, as in many other economically underdeveloped countries, the translation of the economy into monetary terms will in time create a need for ballot boxes.

The Effects of Revolution

In former days the councils of notables were essentially councils of elders. The most striking feature of the new Vietnamese communal organizations in the Communist controlled areas is the prominence in them of young men. "Since 1945," according to Pierre Gourou, "armed adolescents have replaced the peaceful councils of notables." "This," he adds, "is not necessarily an improvement." No, but it is a fact, and its historical antecedents are worth examining.

World War II, the Japanese occupation, and most of all the Vichy-inspired reforms, although markedly conservative, instead of turning back the tide of history, succeeded only in accelerating the course of events in Viet Nam. The French seem to have attempted to adapt the Vichy "national revolution" to the Vietnamese monarchy by linking Maurras with Confucius. The Japanese, on the other hand, apparently were disgruntled because Admiral Decoux, by holding out the prospect of a united Indochina, diverted Viet Nam from participating in the war of "Asian liberation" and from taking much interest in the "Greater East Asia Co-Prosperity Sphere." In those days Vietnamese youth was arrayed in serried ranks under French guidance to the tune of "Marshal Pétain, we are here." This mass training of youth has since been utilized by the revolutionaries, who found their cadre among the former members of the Vichy youth organization.

Vietnamese schoolteachers, as well as some local Catholic priests, seem to have exerted a powerful influence on events. Just as elementary-school teachers in France are overloaded with extracurricular duties, so in French-governed Viet Nam instructors have usually been overworked and underpaid. Their education enabled them to criticize the traditional institutions of their country without, however, giving them sufficient understanding of the economic and historical bases of rural society. These teachers were entrusted, in the name of the Marshal, with the task of preparing the youth for what Vichy termed "the national revolution." Thus, owing partly to French initiative, elements of a popular revival were assembled in the intimacy of the Vietnamese countryside, behind the protective hedges of the villages.

Combatant groups would be very much mistaken if they should imagine that they have singlehandedly introduced a new phase in their country's history. The cell-like revolutionary committees have undoubtedly played a leading part in the course of events. But several other historical factors—some of them local in character and certain others dependent on Franco-Vietnamese intercourse—

have contributed to the same end result. These factors the Vietnamese should keep in mind when the time comes for them to tackle the classic problem involved in the demobilization of any resistance force.

Perhaps nothing blocks the solution of any and all issues more hopelessly today than the belief held by each of the opposing groups that it can control the future course of events only if it retains sufficient power to be able to destroy its adversary if it should choose to do so. This attitude suggests that even the much-desired termination of the military conflict may exacerbate rather than ease political difficulties. Regardless of what group may in the future enjoy a majority in the Vietnamese government, the position of the opposition, whether it is rightist or leftist in nature, will be of critical importance in the evolution of a comprehensive national policy. A leader of the Democratic Republic of Viet Nam once remarked to Paul Mus, "Nothing can prevent us from executing those whom we regard as traitors." While such sentiments may be permissible in wartime, peace—and first of all peace in the villages, without which peace in the country as a whole is unthinkable—will require a somewhat different approach.

In the interests of peace it will be necessary for Westerners, as well as for the conservative Vietnamese, to desist from efforts to pacify the country by re-establishing traditional village institutions as part of a political and military "security network"—a concept which, as has been noted, is economically and socially obsolete. A country which, partly with Western inspiration and assistance, has begun to realize its modern potentialities cannot be pacified merely by being forced to contemplate its past. A transitional link in the national development (which has perhaps been promoted rather than interrupted by the revolution) might possibly be found in the revolutionary phase itself. Traditional rural society contained a multitude of specialized social groups—councils and subcommittees, classes based on age, neighborhood groups, and literary, religious, corporative, women's, and children's associations. Here perhaps is where the two worlds—the old and the new—have a point of contact.

In certain respects the "revolutionary" front imitates the traditional structure of society by proliferating groups, not only of workers, soldiers, and peasants, according to the hallowed formula, but also of women, children, old people, merchants, former soldiers, and the like. These associations originated as a network of cells, an aspect which they will not easily shed as long as the war continues. But in peacetime they are more likely to become more broadly and normally representative of rural society. They have already helped to establish the technique of elective institutions in the villages, and have played an instrumental part in the recruiting of local administrative committees. They may help to satisfy the Vietnamese predilection for a civil hierarchy, henceforth based on ability instead of on privilege.

A vigorous resistance party, aware that the economic development of the Vietnamese masses is less advanced than its own leftist doctrine, might wish to impose an autocratic government on the people without reference to their inclinations. Or, alternatively, Vietnamese of all political complexions might come together in agreement that their people, in the course of its long and painful history, has demonstrated enough good qualities to warrant its deciding its own future without having first to mortgage it. The latter course, however, will draw on all the capabilities of the country in all their diversity; if a joint effort is attempted, certain compromises will be necessary. In sum, therefore, it is likely that Viet Nam will be unable to realize all its potentialities until a sufficient number of former notables have rejoined the innovators in the village councils, whatever the shape and nature of the national government.

5.

The Political Consequences of Vietnamese Concepts of Society

Viet Nam is a certain way of growing rice, of living in common on a rice diet, and of asking heaven to protect your harvest just as it did your ancestors'. Viet Nam is a piece of luck solicited, administered, and experienced in common. It is a country that presents us with a dual paradox, because for the Vietnamese everything is religion down to the simplest acts; yet they seem to have no religion in our sense of the word. Magic, religion, ethics, temporal power: our categories are not theirs; for them one sole fact is involved. This unity of life the Vietnamese call "common fortune," and to them it means that which makes them Vietnamese.

Within Viet Nam's former traditional society this whole system of beliefs was embodied in the Emperor, whose ritual acts symbolized the spiritual feelings of the Vietnamese. For example, the Emperor was the Prime Plowman who each year used to "deconsecrate" the precious rice land by opening the first furrow. This annual ceremony was preceded by an imperial procession into the rice fields, all of which gave the village people a sense of the spiritual significance of their travail. Government in traditional Viet Nam was thus inseparable from religion; together they were formed in accordance with the human geography required to cultivate rice. Indeed, government was the spiritualization of this human rhythm of growing rice.

While the Emperor sanctified all action, either by ordaining it or controlling it, he did not execute action. On the contrary the Sino-Vietnamese ideal was a sovereign wise enough to rule without moving. Instead, he kept "his hands hanging and his clothing undone"—he ruled through the purity of his example. Because the Emperor's role was so vital to the unity of Vietnamese society, the elimination of his imperial authority during French colonial rule threatened the very foundation of Viet Nam's tenuous social order. No longer was there anyone to perform the ritual ceremonies that gave meaning to a cycle of life geared to the annual production of rice. But despite the absence of a ritual and governmental super-structure over the country, the spirituality of the earth and the heavens continued to permeate the minds of the people. They felt that there would be an imminent resumption of customary behavior in some new political and spiritual hierarchy.

The Vietnamese idea of spirituality is usually expressed by the word *linh* (*ling* in Chinese), which denotes a supernatural and celestial power. The Chinese character for the word associates it with signs for lightning and rainfall. Corresponding to *linh* (or cosmic spirituality) is *tinh* (*ching* in Chinese), which is a more human aspect of spirituality, one that comes from the soil and expresses its essence: its determining sign in Chinese characters is that of rice. Thus in the depths of the Vietnamese consciousness this word evokes the feeling of a harmonization of the earth, the heavens, and the ancestors that takes form in the state religion of the country. Offerings of the first fruits of the peasant world—the rice that is burned sacrificially on the altar or the drinking of distilled rice—express the quintessence of the earth that produced it. This rice is permeated—as the earth is—with the soul of the ancestors who lie buried near the fields where it was produced. Here in Viet Nam is a religion of rice. Here in Viet Nam is a sociology of rice.

The Pattern of Life in the Mekong Delta Breaks with Vietnamese Traditions

The rice lands of the Mekong Delta in southern Viet Nam, which were opened up to cultivation during the early part of the twentieth century, do not fit into this traditional state religion and sociology. By contrast the religious sovereignty of Hué, which became the imperial capital in 1802, was still appreciable in central Viet Nam in the years before 1945, and even enjoyed vestigial prestige in the north. But such a sense of spiritual identity ceased to be strong in Cochin China (southern Viet Nam) after it fell under French control during the years 1863–67. The principal reason for this spiritual decline was the emergence of a new pattern of land tenure. Through the enterprise of French hydraulic engineering vast new tracks of previously uncultivatable land were opened up for rice growing in the delta of the Mekong River. Yet, instead of being made available as small plots to individual peasant producers in the traditional manner of Vietnamese migration into new areas, this land was sold to large landowners as a means of rapidly recouping the cost of hydraulic engineering projects. As a result of this decision an upper class with wealth based on vast landholdings arose for the first time in Vietnamese society.

After three or four generations these great landowning families became very closely identified with French ways of living. They sent their sons to the Sorbonne, to the École Polytechnique, or to law and medical schools in Paris, Marseilles, and Montpellier. Along with their collections of Chinese porcelains and jade one could find that these families—not only in Saigon but also in the Mekong Delta towns like Vinh Long and Ben Tre—had wine cellars which testified to a taste formed at leisure in Paris. Such changes in taste usually went along with the adoption of French nationality. Not that these Vietnamese renounced their own nationality; it was just a change in status to draw near to us. Yet the consequence of this wealth was that the new lands of the Mekong Delta were cultivated by a half-proletarianized labor force that had no title to the land it worked. With the exception of two small spots on the map of Tonkin (northern Viet Nam)—up near the coal mines of Dong Trieu and Hon Gay and the cotton mills of Nam Dinh—these latifundia (vast tracts of land) of the Mekong Delta were the only part of the country where something resembling what orthodox Marxism calls prerevolutionary conditions were being prepared.

Now Viet Nam is best understood as a network of villages set in the midst of small parcels of cultivated rice land. The owner-cultivators of these parcels make up the villages, although a certain portion of these lands are held in communal trust by the village as a means of providing for social welfare. But this traditional pattern of settlement is hard to find in the Mekong Delta. According to the geographer Charles Robequain, "Instead of large villages distributed at almost equal distances in the rice fields as in the rest of Viet Nam there are long rows of houses stuck to rectilinear canals." This striking contrast in the way the Mekong Delta has been settled is only one of the differences that set it apart from the rest of the country, yet it reflects another more profound factor: the radical contrast in the pattern of landowning.

The geographer Pierre Gourou has made a concise study of these factors and his statistical report is startling. Out of the 6,000,000 inhabitants of the Tonkin Delta there were 965,000 landowners before 1940, while in the Mekong Delta there were only 255,000 landowners out of 4,000,000 inhabitants. This meant that in the northern delta there were nearly twice as many landowners per capita as there were in the south. According to the local statistics in Tonkin the small landowners—those who had less than 1.8 hectares of cultivated land—owned the greatest amount of land and numbered 869,000; those with middle-sized holdings (from 1.8 to 3.6 hectares) amounted to 60,000 persons, and the large landholders having over 36 hectares were only 250 in number.

The Mekong Delta province of Bac Lieu offers a vivid contrast to this situation in Tonkin: in the south the situation was just the reverse of that in the north; the large landowners had the greatest amount of land while the small landowners had the least. In the south the large landowners—those controlling more than 50 hectares each—were only 9.6 percent of the total number of landowners; yet, they owned nearly 65.5 percent of the cultivatable land in the province. Thirty-two percent of the land in the province belonged to middle-sized landowners or those who had 5 to 50 hectares and they composed 48.3 percent of the total landowners in Bac Lieu. Finally, those classified as small landowners because they had less than 5 hectares were 38 percent of all landowners but had to share only 3.3 percent of the land in the province. Since only about 6 percent of the population had any land at all, this left a body of tenants and workers who were the beginnings of a proletariat.

Why has the Mekong Delta developed in a way that is so out of character with the rest of Viet Nam? The answer is to be found in the fact that the virgin lands of the delta were salty and, in order to become usable, required a complicated and costly irrigation system, which only French hydraulic engineering was capable of constructing. Once they were cleared and irrigated, these vast new uninhabited lands were a spectacular resource for the French colonial administration. But in order to capitalize on this resource and recoup the cost of developing it, the colonial government sold these lands in large tracts to French companies and Vietnamese landowners. Since these owners could not work the land themselves and since they had little incentive to provide mortgages for small landowners, they set up a tenancy system for the cultivation of their newly acquired property.

Because this system resulted in a different kind of settlement pattern, in which the village and its institutions were relatively less cohesive units than in previous Vietnamese migrations, the principal social consequence of the opening up of new land was not only to create a new class of extremely wealthy landowners but also to produce a rootless and restless peasantry. While the landowners were inevitably staunch supporters of French rule, the rootless peasants were not, and when their chance came they expressed their protest in a violent uprising in 1940–1941. This Communist-led revolt was but a precursor of the more lasting effects of the unusual settlement of the Mekong Delta.

As described by Charles Robequain, the more immediate effects of this pattern of ownership in the Mekong Delta were that:

> The cultivation of the land is no longer a direct concern of the family; it is done . . . through the intermediary of the tenant farmers, or *ta dien,* who have to pay a specific amount of their crop as rent. These penniless farmers, who are often unstable and anxious, receive advances in money and grain from the landowners. And the landowner counts on the interest from such loans as much if not more than he does on the progressive improvement of his rice fields—here the possession of land is, above all, a speculation.

Usury—that endemic disease among the Vietnamese—turns up yet again.

Another striking indication of the contrasts between the Mekong Delta and the rest of Viet Nam has been the amount of land devoted to communal ownership. Since the purpose of such land is to provide funds from the rice yield for village welfare, the amount of communal land is a good, though approximate, index of social cohesion. Pierre Gourou noted in 1940 that communal lands comprised 20 percent of the cultivated area of Tonkin and 26 percent in Annam but only an astonishingly low 2.5 percent in Cochin China. Such figures reveal that the traditional equilibrium of Vietnamese society has been drastically upset in the area of most recent settlement in southern Viet Nam. Villages there do not share the same capacity for social cohesion and social action that villages in other parts of Viet Nam possess.

As Gourou points out:

> For the very large proletariat of Cochinchina where there is only one landowner for every fifteen people[1] it would seem to be a definite advantage to have what little existing communal land there is broken up into private plots. But obviously the habit of renting those communal lands for purposes of social welfare would have to be done away with and this reform would be desirable only if those people in the village actually cultivated the land and made a part of their harvest available for village welfare. At the present time (1940) this goal appears unattainable because big landowners are the ones who far too often are renting the communal lands and then subletting them to the *ta dien* for usurious profits.

Did the French colonial administration allow this beginning of proletarianization to take place just to please the big Vietnamese landowners who were becoming increasingly Francophile? If this were the case it was against the constant warnings and all the best advice from French agricultural experts. From 1946 onward, these

1. Assuming an average of five members per family, only one family in three in the Mekong Delta would have had its own land to work. A situation in which two-thirds of the families were dependent on rented land for their livelihood was a sharp break with Vietnamese traditions in land tenure and social structure.

French experts attempted to change the pattern of land tenure in southern Viet Nam by helping people to acquire their own land and by providing the small farmer-landowners with assistance to avoid the trap of usury. It is rather significant that the agrarian reforms carried out in the zones held by the Southern Committee of the Viet Minh in the late 1940's seem to have been very similar to those proposed by French experts. Yet on both sides the state of war has made attempts at agrarian reform both theoretical and precarious.

The Politico-Religious Sects and the Spiritual Instincts of the Landless Peasants in the Mekong Delta

While the Communist party had undeniable success among the people of the Mekong Delta it could not compare in the 1940's and 1950's with the extraordinary expansion of the politico-religious sects that originated there. The best-known of these sects are the Cao Dai, which sprang up in 1926 in Saigon as a spiritualist religion, and the Hoa Hao, a rural-based religious movement launched by the so-called crazy monk, Huynh Phu So. In the mid-1940's the Hoa Haos numbered about a hundred thousand, and though the Cao Daists counted a half million partisans, they could easily double or triple that figure if they included their fluctuating sympathizers. In most of the villages of the western part of the Mekong Delta, Communism has been kept at bay by the strength of these revolutionary, or at least rightist reformist, politico-religious groups. Yet their opposition has not been based so much on a difference of views over the nature of agrarian reform as it has been a clash with Communism as a religious adversary.

When the French annexation of Cochin China cut off southern Viet Nam from the national state religion, it became an area where substitute religions sprang up—often in mystical and prophetic form. Besides their mystical concerns, these new religions adopted a militant attitude toward French interference in Vietnamese society. This intertwining of religious and secular attitudes of the sourthern delta area can be seen in a representative pamphlet of the Cao Daist sect that was published about 1940. It describes in some interesting detail the circumstances that were instrumental in creating the new faith:

> With the triumph of capitalism the old patriarchal structure in southern Viet Nam is falling apart. The Gia Long Code which was essentially anti-individualistic because it recognized only the rights of such collectivities as the family or village was abolished, or almost so. Since individual liberty has been more or less recognized in Cochinchina by new legal codes the result has been that Confucianism has fallen into disrepute. . . . Under such conditions the authority of the father, the husband and the landlord has been more threatened in Cochinchina than in other parts of Viet Nam where the Gia Long Code and Confucianism still hold their power.

Judged from the French point of view Cao Daism would appear to have been an alarming movement. Since the leaders of the sect announced that their overriding goal was the conquest of territorial power and the organization of a governmental administration, the French—in fear of what the Cao Dai might do—exiled their "Pope," Pham Cong Tac, to Madagascar shortly before World War II. But once the war was over they reversed themselves by reinstalling him in his "Holy See" simply because France desperately needed the enthusiasm of his sect's opposition to the Viet Minh. During the Japanese occupation of Indochina the Cao Dai had organized their own army and with it they defended their areas in the Mekong Delta against the Viet Minh when the August Revolution of 1945 began. And after the French forces returned to Cochin China they found the Cao Dai a natural ally against the Viet Minh rather than a nationalistic opponent.

The French were particularly interested in the so-called Confucian branch of the Cao Dai, which was especially successful in expanding its organization among the villages of Cochin China. It claimed to have direct communications with a supernatural power that gives orders to men—including Westerners. Here was a power that was superior to French laws and military strength and that might intercede on behalf of Cao Dai followers among the Vietnamese. From such mysticism there arose a sect comparable politically to a kind of Moslem fanaticism. It produced a religious and political hierarchy among the Cao Dai based on the feeling that "the only duty the mass of the believers have . . . is that of following the ethics and rules of behavior pointed out to them by the ruling committee of Cao Daism."

In Viet Nam when a community listens to the voice of the spirits and at the same time is formed into armed regiments, one can expect the most violent and disconcerting reactions in time of war. True, Cao Daism claims to be a renewed form of Buddhism, and the teachings of Buddha condemn, in principle, all violence; but it is also true that throughout Chinese as well as Vietnamese history there is evidence of mystical Buddhist sects that provided tough fighters. The Buddhist books that describe Cakyamouni's victory over passion and error as represented by the devil, Mara, or death give us some understanding why battalions of Buddhist monks follow banners on which they have written, "Let us master the devils," as they march cheerfully off to civil wars ready to conquer their cosmic enemy—in other words, their earthly opponent.

Religion as the Sign of a New Epoch in Vietnamese Politics

The Cao Dai is not a true religion—it is a substitute religion. In the classical civilization of East Asia it is customary and sensible for a religion to sustain everything: society, the state, even the world. Religion is a cosmology. Proclaiming that "the world is going to change fundamentally" is not its last word but its first. Such is the manner in which an Asian religion announced the arrival of a new epoch, even though the popular acceptance of the existence of a new epoch is, inevitably, an uncertain thing. Each Vietnamese waits for a sign of a new era; he tries to figure out what the immediate future will bring. The Vietnamese, who are gamblers, have the profound conviction that life is like turning up a winning card; those who have guessed the winning card correctly will enjoy the fruits of the new epoch while the losers will take nothing. Power will be conferred upon those who express and emulate most satisfactorily the principles on which everything will be reconstructed in the new epoch. The winner's slogan is the same as for us in the West, "We were nothing; let's be everything."

In practice there is considerable political power attached to such expectations of succession. Without meaning any direct harm to the French, Cao Daism was preparing to be everything when its founder, Huynh Phu So, proclaimed the arrival of a Wise King who would reform the universe. Well before World War II, Japanese politicians were singularly better informed about these deep forces than the French were. During their wartime occupation of Viet Nam the Japanese tried to make these politico-religious movements converge under the leadership of the pretender of the imperial throne of the country, Prince Cuong De. He had gone to Japan after its victory in the Russo-Japanese War because he felt that this defeat of a European power was an indication of Japanese leadership in a new epoch in Asia. Despite his efforts to get young Vietnamese to Japan for education and his clandestine political organization in Viet Nam, Cuong De never became accepted as the herald of a new epoch within his own country. Because his popularity was so marginal the Japanese found it necessary to turn to other, indigenous groups for political support of their occupation instead of relying on the man they had cultivated for nearly four decades.

What the French found most disconcerting about this Vietnamese anticipation of the beginning of a new epoch was its implication for the end of colonial rule. But why did France see this as hostility directed against her? It was not so much a conspiracy as it was a bet that one tries to place in time. If the French were to disappear it would mean that heaven had willed it; France must have a successor, and the destiny that takes away French power will give it to that successor. Under such circumstances of inevitability why would Cao Daism, for example, have any ill will toward France? And should the French really have been annoyed that the Cao Dai were preparing for the future? If Frenchmen had understood the game they wouldn't have been irritated. Or have the French regarded their statements about the difference in mentality between themselves and the Vietnamese as mere propaganda? Yet

from their perspective the Cao Dai no more expected to receive
the elements of territorial authority—army, police, customs, etc.—
from France than to have to tear it away by force. It would receive
them only from a supreme authority transcending France and Cao
Daism as well. However, a religion which did not prepare to assume secular responsibilities would not, in Vietnamese eyes, be a
religion at all.

In this moral and political light the direct and deep influence on
the masses by the politico-religious sects, the Hoa Hao and the
Cao Dai, should have caused the French to be more thoughtful.
Does the social and cultural imbalance in the Mekong Delta constitute a prerevolutionary Marxist situation or, on the contrary, is
it an environment favorable for the return of traditional structures
in politics? Could new life be breathed into a traditional monarchy
so that it could claim direct contact with the supernatural? In any
new political departures the evil to be overcome lies in an agrarian
system that diverges from the typical Vietnamese formula: families no longer possess the land they work on; they have been left
with a sense of insecurity and have sought extreme means for their
self-preservation. This impulse clashed with the order French colonial administration had established and which its armed forces,
police, and civil service protected. Thus there is an argument to
be made against us: The French are the ones who sold the land;
through French policies rich families in Viet Nam—who spoke
France's language, sometimes almost forgetting their own, imitated
French ways, and finally adopted French nationality—had created
a situation by which they broke the Vietnamese social contract.

The Vietnamese Concept of Society

The Vietnamese concept of society is not simply that of a contract between men; society does not gather individuals together
according to the logic of Rousseau. The Vietnamese social contract
is an agreement between heaven, the land, and the ancestors,
whose spirit was thought to be embodied in the living generation.
The state was the ultimate instrument of the contract: the Emperor, the image of heaven, in his capital; the governors in their

provinces; the heads of families in their houses, were all one sole entity who were in harmony with the reason of the universe. Through conformity with this hierarchy the contact with the supernatural was direct and assured. Natural calamities were regarded as proof that contact with the supernatural had been lost and that conformity to the social contract had been violated. Individuals had to function within the system; there was no reality for the individual apart from the social contract. There was no individual property; there weren't even any individual rights. People were simply an element in social integration except when they achieved positions of authority. Such positions didn't mean, however, that their share of existence was any more individual; it was the heavenly mandate that had come upon them and that had made them a replica of itself.

Everywhere the concrete facts corresponded to these concepts of society. They were reinforced by all the ways of seeing, speaking, and writing which constituted Sino-Vietnamese civilization. The individual was situated within his family; the families were defined by the village, and when they became rich their assets inevitably reverted to the collectivity. When the French quantified the individual by giving him both a civil status and the idea of individual rights and duties, they destroyed a qualitative harmony made up of exchanges and compensations. They made the individual his own capital and gave him rights that could be opposed to his own family and his village; they armed him, theoretically, against them. But a society is not that easily reformed. In traditional society the individual had only relative rights, but they were fulfilled because, on an average, the system assured everyone a piece of land, and the communal assets helped the village erase the most glaring inequalities.

In the Mekong Delta, however, where the pattern of land tenure and social structure broke with long-standing tradition, the individual who was provided with absolute rights by the West found himself faced with empty rights from the viewpoint of customary values. He had the rights of a salaried man and this, according to Vietnamese civilization, does not constitute a person. These individual rights have no juridical value because they are not a function, a responsibility, or a replica of the heavenly mandate, and they cannot represent the will of heaven because, as one realizes immediately, they benefit only the very few. Riches now are placed in bank accounts and have left the community; the rich people live in cities and the villagers encounter only the managers. The circulation of assets, which had once been assured within a closed circle by the community spirit, no longer takes place. "Face" is elsewhere: Western individualism passed that way, creating cities and a new world.

One cannot expect these simple people who live in the villages of southern Viet Nam to be able to make a correct economic analysis of the situation that the French colonial administration has created. For example, they cannot see that in the opening up of new lands in the Mekong Delta there was a requirement for machines and capital which traditional Vietnamese culture could not have provided. Instead they see themselves as dispossessed; emptied of substance. They see what for them are fabulous fortunes building up at their expense and beyond their reach. Although more exasperated, the attitude of the village communities toward such fortunes is the same as that toward village families who claim to be rich on their own account. There is a deep-rooted conviction that such behavior can never bring luck and that the vengeance of heaven is on its way.

It is by no means certain that this state of annoyance is everywhere leading to Marxism; local agrarian movements have, on the contrary, favored the politico-religious sects. They claim that the misfortune of the times is due to a loss of contact with the supernatural, since the mediating apparatus of the Confucian State was destroyed and not replaced except for precarious administrative arrangements between men. Here is where spiritualism comes into the picture: the Cao Daist mediums with simple improvised means have re-established the communication, and listening to them means listening to heaven again. But beyond such direct practices this religion of systematic opportunism has built itself up into a hierarchy which claims it will re-establish the ancient state institutions once the power is conferred by heaven. Since the French secular system failed to provide such a replacement one may suppose that within this new politico-religious structure, the village as an institution will again be in harmony with the cosmos and will regain its traditional efficiency. Communism offers no guarantees of this nature.

The values that attach the Vietnamese peasant to the soil he tills were created through a host of historical circumstances. First of all the peasants personally and directly took hold of the land by every means possible; they evicted the Chams and Cambodians, or supplanted the previous Vietnamese occupants who had disqualified themselves by their rebelliousness, and reclaimed the land for cultivation. Then came the integration of their territorial conquest into the regular system—the network of villages that humanize the landscape and are guaranteed by the supernatural. The ultimate value of this village network is, of course, religious; such districts of human habitation are paralleled by a world of ancestors who constantly watch over the life of the living and guarantee it. The state in effect was a supernatural body of prestigious persons. This kind of equilibrium is what the Cochin Chinese peasant milieus are leaning toward today, because they are still led by a strong traditionalist instinct. They reacted against French rule because they found themselves separated from both this communal and spiritualist stabilization.

If it is true that the whole conflict began against France because of the individual Vietnamese's instinct for a recovery of social cohesion, then what is the meaning of possible choices for the future? Considered from a traditionalist point of view France's action in the virgin lands of the Mekong Delta has incurred two serious reproaches. France made the individual into a political principle to the detriment of collective groups; in French theory it was the individual and no longer the collectivity that became the legal and economic unit. Yet at the same time France dispossessed that individual of everything the collectivity had once put at his disposal, thus the only ones who benefited from this fallacious emphasis on the rights of the individual were a few clever people who became French clients, the rich upper classes. Moreover, the resulting proletarianization, which is the most obvious characteristic of the system and the one most open to criticism, was due directly to France's failure to recognize the religious functions of communal unity. In Confucian society the ritual order, good behavior, and conformity to the past—that is, to the cosmic structure —within families and within the state regularizes the order of the seasons, the sun, and the rain.

Seen in this way a society is a vast and perpetual incantation of the universe. Man does not act. He officiates—well or badly, and certainly badly if he is not enlightened. The classical and canonical books were his code, and in them he found the conduct each one was to follow so that the individual might be in harmony with his family and village and that the empire might be at peace.

6.

The Vietnamese Elite on the Eve of Revolution

When revolution finally broke out in Viet Nam in 1945 it did not come as a conflict between the French and the people of the rural areas. With regard to the things that the peasants considered important—the "face" of provincial authority, the installation of communications, public safety, and customary law—the French were close enough to the peasants to be accepted. But they remained too distant from the peasants with regard to the things the French considered important—modern institutions and status as individuals. The peasants felt that France was not offering them a way out of their condition now that their Confucian past was over and done with. Consequently, there were no elements of real fusion or of rivalry between the French and the country people. The relationship might be called a symbiosis that never involved them fundamentally (indeed, France never reached them fundamentally). Moreover, they sensed that the relationship would have to fall apart just when they, in all their simplicity, were getting to know its advantages.

Badly informed about the modern productive framework that was required by the type of objects, actions, and men the French were sending them, the peasants tended more and more to convince themselves that they could keep those advantages without also paying the price for the colonial administration which had first instituted them. The price did not lie merely in the burdensome taxes that the rural people were already being asked to pay. Instead they were being asked to commit themselves to a new way of life with only sparse preparation for the transition; they were being asked to undertake an act of faith. Among the villagers of Viet Nam the French were dealing with peasants whose decision on a path to the future would have been crucial for a continuation of French influence in the country, but on whom they could not have counted to get up on the stage and play an active part with them. Doubtless the handicap of the anti-Communist Bao Dai government, 1948–1954, was that it inherited this ambiguous state of affairs. What would the people of the countryside become committed to?

In contrast to this distance between them and the people of the villages, the French were in close touch with an increasingly large group of Vietnamese intellectuals. These men played around with France, pro and con, because the training they had received in French institutions had dislodged them from Vietnamese culture. Their cultural references became the same as those of the French; having left the world of geomancy they calculated everything they thought or did according to geography, sciences, and techniques. They came to see life as a measured universe where there are no more dark corners left for spirits who see the world differently from everybody else. But despite this closeness to Western culture, it is this French-trained Vietnamese elite that led the opposition to France in Viet Nam. How is it, then, that they were so close culturally yet so opposed politically? In great part the violence of revolution has stemmed from the military and political aftereffects of the French defeat by Japan in 1940 and the five years of Japanese occupation of Indochina. Because of this defeat they saw French weaknesses, and from the Japanese as well as France and America they acquired the weapons to exploit them.

But even more important, perhaps, is the fact that confronting France within the Vietnamese classes that are qualified to govern was a transitional generation with no inner psychological balance. They were led to extremes by that congenital tension which can result in violent action that sweeps everything away or, alternatively, can be manifested in apathy and indecision. This is the behavior of a nervous person; he has within him great resources for thought and action but one is very often wrong about him because his actions are so unpredictable. His mental indecision and almost physical torpor are deceptive signs; they often indicate that he is preparing for some explosive action in the future. Because the French cultural façade of this complex personality structure is so misleading it cannot be easily understood without reference to the Vietnamese cultural world from which it emerged.

Traditionally, the Individual Existed Within a Collective Unit

In traditional Vietnamese society every individual act carried out in a collective unit—family, clan, village, etc.—was governed and evaluated by relatives and neighbors. They judged a person's behavior on the basis of his "sacralization" or "deification" of life. Within the norms of the collective unit the individual always had his assigned part to play. During celebrations of the change of seasons, events in the calendar of agricultural labor, and family events, the purpose of traditional rituals was to consecrate the mundane passage of life. Every ritual action of the performers was preceded by an announcement, spoken aloud, of the gestures they were about to make. This was like an oracle predicting in advance the behavior prescribed to achieve harmony with the supernatural: through appropriate behavior there would be a good harvest, a prosperous year, a successful life. Through the behavior of its members each collectivity sought to establish harmony between itself and the divine power of nature; thus each village, each clan, each family continually prompted the individual's mind and governed his actions.

The problem for the individual was *to know* what was expected by the collectivity. The approval of the group was the invariable condition for action, and this was not just superficial approval arising from some whim or impulse but an expression of constitutional approval, as it were. When disapproval was incurred, it carried a power effective enough to maintain the basic character of the collectivity. When there was approval, the sanction of opinion became the very reason for individual existence: an individual had achieved harmony with nature and his fellows, he had been integrated into the world, and he could expect good luck.

For those who did not achieve this harmony there was death, a religious and civil death. The French were constantly surprised at the number of cases in which loss of face resulted in murder and, even more, in suicide. This violence occurred because "face" is not just another word for vanity or social pretension; it is the very character of one's being. Through the sociological mechanism of the individual's integration into a group and the group's integration into the world of society and nature, there is a self-realization and self-awareness that frees one from the doubts, the violence, and the depressions that characterize introverted and subjective ways of living.

In the extreme climate in the tropical zone, which has such a strong effect on the human organisms, a race endowed with more nerves and intelligence than muscle and bone finds stability in this kind of collective behavior. The explosion set off by a scene between women in the street or a fit of defiance and anger in a young child—real tragedies acted out right on the sidewalk—give some idea of all that is smoldering under the convention of civility and show why it is necessary. However, the more society sets up barriers of behavior around individual spontaneity the more that spontaneity, in yielding, builds up and is in danger of bursting forth. Here is a society under tension; one in which conformity has to be increased in order to counter a situation that it itself has developed. The society must manage the reactions of individuals caught between general rules of conduct and the latent human intolerance toward any kind of rules.

If one adds the fact that the decorum—that protection against individual drive—was dependent on Chinese tradition whereas individual spontaneity was a combination of human reactions and indigenous tradition, one gets a broader notion of the historical tension under which an organized society of village people lived in Viet Nam. Here the mental landscape corresponds to the physical landscape that frames it: the rivers have a seasonal exuberance and must be dammed; the dams that are built up also raise—through an inevitable physical effect—the river bed; they must therefore be made a bit higher. Pushed to the limit this picture becomes one of catastrophe. Perhaps the same may be said of Vietnamese formalism. This tradition set local society in Viet Nam within an established though completely alien order—one which was assuredly welcome and protective for the individual within it, but one which was loaded with latent violence once a crisis arose.

In Europeanizing the Vietnamese intellectuals and accepting them into their ranks the French both shattered their mental apparatus—their traditional conception of the world—and put their behavior outside the sociological context in which they were raised. The classical Vietnamese society was no more abstract or theoretical than that of France; it did not live on ideas alone. Its most philosophical conceptions could never be separated from the economic, political, administrative, and family structures that made them meaningful. Adapting these social structures to a view of the cosmos meant that the resulting cosmology became the doctrine of the intellectual elite.

Once the belief in these ideas was taken away, the social system fell apart. In the kind of traditional sociological structure found in Viet Nam, the participants must do more than accept the ideas it is based upon as useful. They have to think they are true. Indeed, such is the technique of all propaganda. Therefore, the Vietnamese culture tradition aimed as much at convincing people as at schooling them; its perpetual internal propaganda was conducted through ideas, rites, gestures, and images as conveyed by ideographical characters in the Chinese writing system.

Only by thinking in such ritualistic forms did one really feel oneself—in traditional Vietnamese culture—as self-redeemed by its harmony with men and the universe. As a result of this harmony one enjoyed "face" and felt assured of luck among men. One could also feel assured of luck in the bosom of the universe, which was either a piece of good fortune for the individual or a mandate from heaven for those who exercised the authority of the empire. To grasp the social force that came into play from these ritual beliefs we must understand that the luck the peasant felt within himself or appealed to in order to make headway in his humble work was for him of the same nature as the fortune which graced the Emperor and made him Emperor. Therefore, the village rites were a reproduction of the state ceremonial cult, cut down to local proportions; all rites were those of the state, and the state was man's constant assurance with regard to a potentially hostile nature. It was precisely in this situation that the French found the Vietnamese in the seventeenth century just as they had been throughout their history: defending their environment against the forests and swamps and vying with the weather for their crops.

The Traditional Psychology of the Vietnamese

It is not a paradox to say that the history of Viet Nam can be seen in the landscape of the country. Moreover, the traditional psychology of the Vietnamese is not constructed any differently: it is identical with the picture of nature as transformed by the sheer force of men. But when they lose their harmony with heaven, the latent power that is always within them is ready to destroy and obliterate their handiwork. Isn't this actually the very same image of natural tension that is conveyed by the popular belief in the duality of man? Each of us bears within himself two souls, or rather two groups of souls. One group is below and rises up within us from the soil along with the sustenance we draw from it; these are vegetative souls. But having boldly anticipated the most modern psychological theories, the Vietnamese believe that these earthly souls constitute not only our bodies but also our mental functions. They are our share of the earth. Depending on their conduct men also have a share of heaven, and in its purest form this spirit of heaven is reason. Consequently, the Vietnamese believe the meaning of reason to be a man's having become aware of the harmony within himself and among his fellows.

Because of its social dimension this type of reason was not separate from the political structure of the state in traditional Viet Nam. A society of reasonable beings was one established in conformity with cosmic laws to shape the lives of its members according to a pattern dictated by the commonly shared view of the cosmos. A reasonable being was one who became aware of this system and of his place in it. That is why the Confucian doctrine which became the cornerstone of the classical Vietnamese world was not metaphysics but sociology—a sociology integrated into nature. Within Confucian doctrine the traditional personality of the Vietnamese was a personality committed in advance, a personality which became aware of itself in that commitment. It was absolutely and fundamentally bent on social order. Mr. So-and-so, son of So-and-so, born in such-and-such a village, in such-and-such a district, in such-and-such a province: that's how Vietnamese life was determined.

The structure of the traditional personality in Viet Nam was thus a transposition and a reflection of his social and geographic background. When society conquers the obscure forces of nature and disciplines them with the help of heaven into a geographic form, it transforms the human landscape and each individual found in it. Nothing can dominate these measureless forces of nature except the measure that society puts collectively into things: henceforth, man would be able to create within himself the order he sees around him by exercising his reason. Ritual behavior under collective discipline and supervision are what instruct him and break him in.

Understood in this way "face" is more than the stirring of obscure passions which tear you apart; it is the assurance of appropriate behavior. And the discipline of the system lies in the behavior of the intellectual elite, which brands every action and every thought with complete dependability and absolute sincerity. Through a conviction of the truth of the system the individual is permanently saved from himself; he realizes himself as others see him and not as he sees himself introspectively. This is not a game of vanity. It is a game of life and death. Everything is in it together, and the rule of the game was none other than Confucian society itself; but the system disappeared along with the cosmological myth.

The Transitional Generation Within the Vietnamese Elite

The legitimacy of any intellectual elite lies in the popular acceptance of its arts, letters, rites, and all the social and academic decorum that goes with their intellectual lives. In Viet Nam's former traditional society there were skeptics among the intellectual elite, but their existence did not influence the practical workings of institutions. The people, of course, knew very little about such aberrations; it was enough that they believed in the system itself. Don't we of the Western world constantly act in accordance with the discipline of the sciences, even though our only knowledge of them is through intermediaries? Yet we apply their principles daily, from steering a car to taking medicines that are prescribed to us. And if we ceased to believe in the scientific intellectual system, our world would inevitably suffer.

Such is the problem of the transitional generation within the Vietnamese elite. To those who became French pupils and who eventually became French rivals, it was obvious that the system of the Taoist and Buddhist-Confucian world could not survive the shock of positive science. What view of the world can a Vietnamese prince—a fragment of the will of heaven on earth— have when he teaches at the École Polytechnique? If this Vietnamese generation has the time to write its memoirs, the future will obtain some unusual information on the balance between Eastern and Western civilizations and on the spirit shared between them.

In this transitional period the separation of the two worlds is made more distinct for the new Vietnamese elite by the use of the French language for all studies and research. The logical system of Western sciences was presented historically to the Vietnamese in the form and through the grammatical apparatus of the French language, itself the residue of centuries of effort toward knowledge and application—a residue that Viet Nam will have inherited at the beginning of its new life. In 1945, Paul Mus realized that several of his childhood friends who had received their doctorates in law or medicine in Paris were unable to draw up in their own language a simple leaflet giving their compatriots a sincere perspective on the revolutionary events of the time. But deep within themselves an unrivaled power remained attached to certain Vietnamese words, certain elementary expressions that they had learned from their mothers and spoken in the back rooms of the house—even in those places in Cochin China where in the drawing room one spoke French to one's father and his circle of friends.

What is a civilization if not a few words pregnant with meaning? The careers of Mus's Vietnamese friends, the value they put on themselves, and the contributions they felt able to provide, all these were estimated and expressed in French. Their future and that of the nation they had been called upon to build were thus in harmony with Western ideas. But the whole of Viet Nam is also in the few words learned in infancy and only rediscovered with delight and sometimes embarrassment at the end of long studies abroad. Gradually, that expression of family feeling through Vietnamese words and Chinese characters is recalled.

Yet it was not out of nostalgia that one of the most brilliant Vietnamese polytechnicians attempted to compose a dictionary of Sino-Vietnamese characters applied to modern science. Such an attempt to convey the form of Western sciences in the Vietnamese language is not chauvinism. Mus's subjective impression in grasping something of the inner drama experienced by so many of his childhood Vietnamese friends is that this is their attempt at reunification. Two slices of their lives, childhood and maturity; two forms of logic, one affective the other rational; and two languages clashed within them. Making Vietnamese the language for everything was an attempt to pull oneself together.

However, Mus had no doubt that the Vietnamese language is insufficient for the tasks it will be asked to perform. Moreover, a reliance on the Vietnamese language would mean that one more bond between the Vietnamese and the French—and certainly the most fruitful one—would be shattered. And yet this duality of language and logic is so similar to the traditional duality upon which the Vietnamese have constructed their undeniable intellectual achievements. Within the clash, the idea is created. By probing the historic antecedents of their Vietnamese associates and going to the source of their finest achievements, perhaps the French would discover an equilibrium conciliating two opposing terms. In earlier centuries the contrast was between the language of Chinese social philosophy and the language of the home

—that linguistic cradle of the Vietnamese. In the past as today the fundamental dichotomy between the weak and the strong exists in Vietnamese life. The *yin* is complementary to the virile and officialized *yang!*

Although in every village one finds graduates of Franco-Vietnamese schools, the problem of language is not the primary cultural problem of those who live in the countryside. If only because of the disappearance of jobs for the traditionally educated and the discontinuation of the great ceremonies of the official religion, everyone is aware that there is no longer a Confucian state as an intermediary between the village and the universe. The instinctive reaction to this awareness could only be that of withdrawing into the village communities. The village society was saving the base of its cosmological pyramid and waiting for heaven to declare itself by restoring the complete structure. "Wait and see" has been the watchword of the people of the Vietnamese villages; it is a phrase not altogether foreign to the West.

But the Vietnamese intellectuals could not wait. The origin of the conflict they lead was implied in the very nature of France's colonial presence in Viet Nam. When the Confucian universe and the religious state fell to pieces under the impact of French culture and secular institutions the peasants found themselves reduced to the social infrastructure and under French policy, that infrastructure remained solid and secure. However, it was lacking a superstructure that might have linked the infrastructure to a new age. The Vietnamese elite trained among the French, but at first only as subordinates in secondary jobs. They found themselves associated with a superstructure that did not belong to them and uprooted them from their basic traditions; for them it was the infrastructure that was wanting.

The French armed those new Vietnamese with an objective science. It replaced a knowledge based on myth, and it is clear that such progress is irreversible. But in supplying them with a cosmic complex of facts and truths which they were unaware of, France did not provide for everything the Vietnamese intelligentsia sought in an intellectual system. The strength as well as the weakness of the traditional elite lay in its commitment; their ideas about the world were never separate from a social constitution interposed between the world and man. That structure—and let no one forget that it was one of the most brilliant and lasting in all the civilizations in the world—was filled with mythical errors about things. Yet it also possessed a deep understanding of man in his physical environment and sociological origins. Such a universe of fables was made for the practical adjustment of men among themselves and to their tasks according to a plan inscribed during the course of centuries. Indeed, this view of the universe freed the individual from his own problems through collective obedience. That one could be educated without being committed to the social order would have been, for Confucius' practical wisdom, the very negation of culture.

On the contrary, the French learn at the Sorbonne about the objective handling of the sciences, which leaves each person with the responsibility for his personal commitment in all political and religious matters. Each individual makes up his own mind about these matters according to what he discovers within himself and according to his family or professional background. French society is mentally organized in such a way as to adapt to the fact of science; but in Viet Nam, on the other hand, the acquisition of European science made the commitment to the traditional order of things an intellectual impossibility. No one goes back to the school of myth when he has seen, or thinks he has seen, to the bottom of it. Moreover, here was a rising Vietnamese generation that no longer spoke the language of the people who constituted the social infrastructure of the country. How could they become the respected cultural elite of a people with whom they could not communicate? Deprived of their historical bonds, how could these young Vietnamese intellectuals find a new social commitment in the intellectual framework with which the French provided them?

The energy so many Vietnamese intellectuals put into their studies and the harvest of doctorates that resulted were, paradoxically, signs of a reaction to French culture. But this reaction also had a disastrous effect on some of Paul Mus's Vietnamese friends; he saw apparently brilliant careers end in suicide because of an incapacity to adapt. This was because the beginning posts in France's colonial society in Viet Nam—even when they were treated on the same footing as the French—did not give these young intellectuals a feeling of being in charge of national property and production. And this was mostly because for them the objective world—which we are able to transcend because of our personal views of it—was not an answer to everything.

Western secular logic has not given the Vietnamese masses and intellectuals the two basic references which their mentality and temperament seek out as support: collective commitment to a social order through every act, every idea, and every word; and social perspective in which rituals situate the individual in cosmic harmony with the world. Because of the strict discipline of Western knowledge those Vietnamese who pursue it are left outside traditional thinking and far from any preconceived ideas of the world. Thus any French-trained Vietnamese intellectual who is predisposed toward Confucianism is led to solitude and desolation.

How understandable that some Vietnamese long suspected their French friends of concealing a secret knowledge of the true laws of nature and, by keeping it to themselves, being able to dominate the world. This is not a figment of the imagination. Paul Mus knew a time when the Vietnamese were trying to figure out what secret recipes for power were hidden behind the French academic curriculum. A little before the outbreak of World War I, he heard in his family's home the French director of a Franco-Vietnamese school tell about a discussion he had just had with his best teacher, a Vietnamese who had a French diploma.

After long and cautious preliminaries the teacher had said: "You know that I'm a disciplined and punctual schoolmaster. Moreover, I have taken sides with you. I approve of the evolution you are trying to bring about in my country and I'm doing all I can to help you. Therefore, you should treat me as a friend and have as much confidence in me as you have in your own people. Why don't you ever give me the real reasons behind what you make me teach? For example, I've been teaching my students for fifteen years that the world turns around the sun. I have always done it as best I could. But after all, even a child has only to look to the east every morning to see that the contrary is true and is as sure as two and two make four. You may be sure that I shall continue faithfully to teach that part of the curriculum. But what I should really like to know is why you make us say that. What result are you expecting? I can't understand what place it has in your way of doing things; don't you have enough confidence in me to tell me your secret?"

This anecdote takes us back to around 1913. Since then the Vietnamese have managed to see through French secrets; they have discovered that the truth is that there is no secret. But under a colonial regime this had implications whose real significance the French didn't fully realize. In the Western intellectual tradition everything was seen in proportion to man. In the Confucian system, on the contrary, there was no individual foundation of privileged participation by the Chinese in truth and power: the Middle Kingdom was the first to receive the will of heaven. What, on the other hand, was the reason for the Europeans' superiority? Of course, the Europeans were much more sure of their superiority in 1913 than they are today. Was it due to a fluke of history that had directed the Greco-Latin heritage toward them and not toward the East? Or was it rather due to the white race's innate superiority, which was a manifestation of its destiny?

As soon as French schools were opened to the Vietnamese each one was in a position to test these theories for himself. These were questions debated at the *lycée* in Hanoi, then at the university and in French professional schools; man to man between fellow Vietnamese and French students. Obviously such human contact resulted in some firm friendships. Paul Mus recalls one friend, Dang Nhu Ich, who in Mus's opinion and that of many others was the most gifted Vietnamese he ever knew. Ich entered the *lycée* at Hanoi from a modest school run by the Friars at Hué. Not having been taught English he learned in one year to speak it as well as those who had been using it since childhood while at the same time taking first place in French, mathematics, and history. He pushed himself so hard in his studies that he died in the effort; it was too much for a human organism fashioned in such a different way.

The Social Distance of French Officials
from the Vietnamese Milieu

An important element of the origins of revolution in Viet Nam would be missing from this picture if we did not take a broader view of the French attitude with regard to the "natives" during the colonial period. Paul Mus's personal experience has provided him with no lack of anecdotes—some dreadful, others moving, many topical—to illustrate the extremes that existed under colonial rule. But what can we conclude from contradictory evidence of this kind? Absolutely nothing. Every country has its share of unbalanced people, killers, and saints, and such extremes should neither be played down nor denied; but neither should they replace the search for historical truth, which will cut them down to size by considering the number of cases that remain unobserved. If the two extremes are recalled here it is in an effort to give some sense of the dimensions of the spectrum in which the Franco-Vietnamese experience occurred.

Having been directly involved in the evolution of French colonial rule, the general feeling Paul Mus had about it is of an anonymous mass of Frenchmen working good-naturedly amidst conditions which from year to year came to resemble, in their minds at least, those at home. With such limited resources for social life, professional tasks took on great importance in proportion to the responsibility involved. "In Europe I was only a number, here I am somebody," said the postman who was improvising a provincial telegraphic network after the big typhoon of 1909. But such increases in status did not bring Frenchmen closer to the Vietnamese environment in which they lived and worked. Instead their heightened sense of superiority served to increase their distance from the Vietnamese milieu and encourage them to withdraw into French-built enclaves.

The appearance of the automobile contributed substantially to this withdrawal. It removed from the native environment even the static and passive value it had had for Frenchmen during the period of sedan chairs and horse-drawn carriages. Henceforth the rice field was not even interstitial; you passed it by without even noticing it, if you didn't want to. It had become an ever-changing panorama generally appreciated for its pictorial value. But for want of using the Vietnamese language, for want of sleeping in the villages as an older generation of Frenchmen had been forced to do—in short, for want of any common human measure within the country—Frenchmen no longer grasped its meaning. At the most they continued to be curious about it, but had less access than ever to its withdrawn and silent spirit.

Revolution did not break out in Viet Nam between the French and the elusive circle of villages which remain the spectators and final arbiters of any political situation. Revolution had to come, and in fact did, between France and the "advanced" Vietnamese— those who had forsaken their own ways of life and tended toward France's. The veiled opposition encountered among the peasants consisted in a struggle to preserve within themselves the right to maintain their cultural distinctiveness from the French. The elite, on the contrary, battled to acquire the right to imitate the French.

During the first campaign for the reoccupation of Cochin China at the end of 1945, with General Leclerc, Paul Mus saw a French polytechnician, Colonel Mirambeau, supervise the repairing of bridges that his fellow student at the École Polytechnique, the engineer Bich, had blown up. The Colonel expressed his esteem for the perfect technique used in destroying the bridges on behalf of the Viet Minh resistance. Beyond the fact of colonial rule, the French and Vietnamese had established a solidarity according to training and profession. The differences in race, far from standing in the way, gave it more value: even the war has not destroyed that entirely.

The statistical realization of the spirit of equality proved to be difficult in French colonial society in Viet Nam from 1920 to 1940; equality was recognized only in individual cases. Paul Mus remembers the period between 1914 and 1924 when the general feeling of the French in Indochina was that universities and professional schools in France were "giving away" diplomas to Vietnamese who snapped them up so easily. It seemed to the colonial mind that the French back home were so very surprised to see a yellow or black man write fairly good French that they handed out *licences*, doctorates, and soon *agrégations* along with the rest. Unfair though this colonial prejudice was in reality, it does serve to explain the attitude Vietnamese students found when they returned to their homeland. They were greeted by French customs officials or policemen as "natives" who had to be taken back in hand. The colonial axiom that "the foremost Annamese would always come after the lowest Frenchmen" was kept alive at the lowest rungs of the colonial officialdom by those who were most defensive about their marginal superiority. But it was at this level that clashes could be most severe and most prejudicial to Vietnamese sensitivity.

In the practical sociology—the French call it good breeding—that governs ordinary European behavior we know that one must never enter into an argument with any kind of law officer, whether a policeman or a customs official. Within his limited functions the officer must keep the full dignity of his authority. If there are further considerations the time to expound them is not while he is performing his official duty. One just goes on one's way. If an appeal is in order one has recourse to a higher authority. But socially and administratively the Vietnamese had no way of going "higher up" to stop an argument with a French colonial officer.

Within a nation itself and especially between two nations the fact of a police force is particularly disagreeable and irritating; no one is more the target of bias or mental reservation than the police. Yet a police force is a necessity even though it is easy for some to condemn it when they live in a social space protected by it. However, we have seen Paris irremediably congested for half a day after one hour of protest work stoppage on the part of the traffic police. Another example is Liverpool, where in the period before World War II a municipal police strike was stopped by the police themselves when they had to face its effects: an almost medieval turmoil due to lack of safety had suddenly spread from the slums to the entire city. And here only cases are mentioned in which the situation had no political implications and did not bring people into political conflict.

In normal times our common sense tells us that the necessity of a police force is one of the servitudes of the social body. But in a normal state of things one can't get a true idea of a country if for subjective reasons one puts the question of a police force at the center of the image. Quantitatively, it is only a secondary element of the community; looking at everything from that point of view is not a good sign. Clashing with a repressive apparatus that protects and serves society means departing from a contract with that society. The historical difficulty begins when there is some doubt as to the contract and its inclusive value. Let us suppose that one party breaks the contract and sets up a program of subversion. By that very fact it leaves the group, and the repression that it may bring upon itself is the result of its own choice. The repression is a political decision signifying that an attempt to crush it would have meant more drawbacks than advantages for the regime. Either the dissenting party was already too strong to clash with it head-on or it was so weak that there was no point in trying to eliminate it and thereby magnify its importance.

But what happens when a party is forced outside common law against its will and is condemned by the rest of society? Here it is the principle of that condemnation which is involved. Is civic spirit the privilege of the regime in power? And what if the power happens to be only local or temporary? If civic spirit is confined to only one side, what proves that it is not confined to the opposition? Therefore we see the polemics and claims directed most particularly to the legitimacy and soundness of the assumption of power—and when there is want of objective criteria about the basis of legitimacy, everything is settled by force.

But when exclusion from politics hinges on the sectarianism of those in power and is no longer a reaction of a legitimate and vital protection of the community, we see how repressive totalitarianism arises. To crown the legitimacy of such a system a charismatic leader is often required; it is a kind of theatrical presentation that restores the principle of authority once there is no hope of convincing people's reason by means of reason. That is how discus throwing is taught in the stadium—by mimicry of the whole man and not by wasting time on a cinematic analysis of his movements. In some of the totalitarian systems the importance given to physical training of the young proves to be more than a mere image: we are faced with a whole system of educating reflexes, a system that dispenses with the higher functions.

A new man is born. Nietzsche bluntly called him a superman; he will be imposed by example. In its explicit form this type of politics sees that its adversaries are put outside the common law —or rather, outside practicing humanity—unless they completely reverse their judgment by submitting. We can't speak here of conversion, at least not in the sense of universal religions which aim at the man in everyone. The only word we can use is submission —the submission of the greatest number within a society. Anyone who yields is spared, but without being allowed to participate; his very capitulation confirms his exclusion. Thus the spirit is broken so that the body may render its services. Such a spiritual humbling of a man recalls the importance of a religious theme as a central reference to each individual. But if a prophetic doctrine is both political and racial, it easily dispenses with theology—or rather it makes theology become flesh by virtue of a public example. "The aim of National Socialism in education," affirmed certain publications of the Third Reich, "is to make 80,000,000 Germans into 80,000,000 replicas of the way Adolf Hitler sees the world and behaves in it."

In contrast with this totalitarianism, what human measure have we in the West given of ourselves to the Vietnamese? And what human measure have the French been able to take of them through the political and social servitude of colonialism?

7.

Marxism and Traditionalism in Viet Nam

What is the Communist solution for Viet Nam's political dilemmas? As a fundamental point in their revolutionary program, the Communists have decided to confiscate large landholdings, especially the estates amassed during French rule, and redistribute them as small plots to landless peasants. Here is a technique that the Communists, following the experience of the party in China, could have been expected to adopt, because it destroys the power base of those identified with the prevailing order and usually wins a popular commitment to a new form of political community. The party's name itself indicates that its ideal is communal, and, in an agricultural society, one of the most conspicuous ways to put such an ideal into practice is by providing land to those who have none. But the traditionalistic Vietnamese mind has had different ideas than those normally held by Marxists about what a communal link should be. According to Vietnamese beliefs, contracts between men and only between men are no foundation for a community.

Since a community in Viet Nam is felt to be a replica and an incantation of the universe, it must be a spiritual community or it doesn't exist. Such a sense of community takes form only through an agreement with heaven and earth, and it must include the symbolic participation of the ancestors whose spirit will permeate the group. When these conditions are unfulfilled there may be a coalescence of different interest groups but no society; there may be an enterprise but no mission. When they do not form a community no more can be expected of such Vietnamese groups than from our own Western forms of organization in Viet Nam.

One of the paradoxes of revolution in Viet Nam is that after various groups opposed to French rule achieved a measure of unity during the August Revolution of 1945, they began to fall out with each other over their differing concepts for a new political community in the country. For instance, the politico-religious sects, the Hoa Hao and the Cao Dai, in their program to remake the country into a traditionalist Vietnamese "empire," not only avoided French ideas but tried to abolish them. The Communists, on the other hand, have incorporated Western principles, and they intend to finish what the West started in Viet Nam by transcending it. Without a doubt, French colonial policies isolated the individual and then, except for a rich upper class, stripped him bare by eliminating the protection of customary law and traditional values, and gave him nothing in return.

Orthodox Marxism's answer to this situation has been to divide up all the existing assets among the individuals who make up society, without there being any reference to the supernatural dimension of their lives. Consequently, the conservative anticolonialists among the politico-religious sects, on the basis of their commitment to a supernatural, have been as opposed to Communism as they have been to French rule. When the French entered into an alliance with these sects in an attempt to forge a common opposition against the Communists, they had to recognize their temporal, or political, authority over wide areas of the Mekong Delta. Obviously, such an alliance was as ambiguous as it was vulnerable.

In trying to win acceptance for their revolutionary leadership in the Vietnamese countryside, the Communists in the late 1940's were not merely seeking a temporary allegiance to their cause that would allow them to eliminate French rule. On the contrary, their goals were more profound. They were laying the foundation for a modern political community which they hoped would lead Viet Nam into the postcolonial world as a united as well as independent country. Since the population of the countryside, where over 80 percent of the Vietnamese lived in 1945, was not united in any political community beyond the village, the prospects for either rallying the peasants against colonial rule or creating a new system of politics was limited. Moreover, the peasants, to the extent that they were anticipating some new indigenous political superstructure in Viet Nam, were expecting a revival of traditional forms of politics. Therefore, if the Communists, or any other modern political leadership, were to create a government capable of succeeding to French rule over all of Viet Nam, they clearly would have to adapt their concept of politics to the traditionalist expectations of the Vietnamese peasants.

In efforts to maintain their influence the French failed to realize what the Communists came to understand about Vietnamese society and adapted themselves to. Most important of all was the fact that Vietnamese concepts of politics have been fashioned over several centuries by the all-powerful action of an intellectual elite whose traditions were adopted from China. The principles and vocabulary of China's history are centered on the idea of a rivalry for power with Heaven as arbiter. Its most classical pattern was established during the Chou dynasty which ended more than two hundred years before the dawn of the Christian era and which witnessed struggles among territorially based feudal states for supremacy over what later became known as central China. As China became more unified under dynastic rule, this competition took the form of feudal groups preparing to become the new dynasty chosen by heaven to succeed to the supremacy of the dynasty whose "virtue," or political effectiveness, was giving out. This was a game of destiny. The stakes were territorial power, and each one placed his bet on a dynastic faction.

Obviously, the Communists could not merely style themselves as a dynastic successor to the French and pretend that they were engaged in a struggle for power along purely traditionalist lines. If they had done so, they would probably have been as ineffectual as the politico-religious sects in the Mekong Delta. Besides, more than any other political movement, the Communists have realized that Viet Nam requires a modern system of politics if the country is to overcome its long-standing weaknesses of disunity and foreign rule. But how could any revolutionary leadership adapt itself to the traditionalist expectations of the peasants, or rather, adapt itself with the effectiveness required to lead the peasants into the modern world, where the politics of mass mobilization and mass participation in political demonstrations and military operations have become the norm? The answer has been found in the traditional concept of "virtue," which is the sign that a prevailing regime enjoys the mandate of heaven, enjoys legitimacy in traditionalist terms.

Proof that a revolutionary regime has the mandate of heaven is the emergence of a new political system that is a complete replacement of the preceding doctrines, institutions, and men in power and that shows itself to be in complete command of the society. Of course, such a stiff test of legitimacy merely indicates that the Vietnamese expect there to be little uncertainty about an insurgent's capacity to govern before there is popular recognition of his being endowed with the mandate of heaven. Since few competitors can fulfill these criteria all at once, the Vietnamese have usually taken a "wait-and-see" attitude toward challengers of the prevailing order. But being gamblers at heart, the Vietnamese have known that they cannot wait too long; otherwise, they may lose their chance to be identified with the winning side. In the critical task of making their choice they look for a sign or an intimation of legitimacy, and the Vietnamese call that sign "virtue."

An effective competitor for legitimacy in an internal conflict in Viet Nam must, therefore, have a program which anticipates and plans for a complete change in the way politics is conducted; which is to say, it must have a new "virtue." The practical necessity of such a requirement lies in the minds of the Vietnamese peasants. In times of turmoil, they look for signs that a new regime has a well-defined concept of order against which they might measure their prospects for local order in the countryside, and consequently, their hopes for personal security. Naturally, if a revolutionary regime is to have a complete program for a new political community, it must, in the process, plan for a communal link with the peasants and a response to their traditional expectations. Because the Communists have gone beyond the partial political programs of their competitors and tried determinedly, though not always successfully, to grapple with the symbols and idiom of traditionalist politics, they have had the most effective revolutionary movement in Viet Nam. Of course, in competing for the mandate of heaven over more than two decades, the Communists have not had to confront an incumbent whose legitimacy has been widely accepted, especially not in the countryside.

Throughout the long years of French colonial rule the Vietnamese were certain that heaven could not indefinitely allow Viet Nam to be administered by men who were born elsewhere. But faced with the evidence of the strength of French rule, they agreed that heaven had assigned an interregnum to the French and this interregnum took its place in the nation's history. Yet the Vietnamese never stopped competing with the French, and this rivalry brought the French into the game with them. Heaven would decide the outcome. And just as the Vietnamese had adapted to French superiority, it was the rules of the game that the French, in turn, would acknowledge the decree of heaven that put an end to their rule. Thus, faithful friends of yesterday turned against Frenchmen when France attempted to reoccupy Viet Nam in 1945. The indignation of the Vietnamese, which was so painful and incomprehensible to their French friends, stemmed from the fact that, for them, France was breaking the contract whereas during the French occupation they had scrupulously carried out its clauses. There was, of course, still a place for the French in Viet Nam as friends under Vietnamese sovereignty but only on the condition that they would recognize the "liberation" of the country.

Perhaps the following story can best illustrate this point. One day in the era before World War II, a mature and experienced Vietnamese who knew the French well, commented to Paul Mus on the devotion with which Frenchmen were carrying out their duties in the colonial administration. Mus knew that several Frenchmen, on their deaths or retirement, had been made patron spirits by rural people. "But why," he asked Mus, "do you want to have authority over us at any price? What are you so impatient about? Your *Karma* had you born in the West. Yet you love this country of Viet Nam and you choose to live here rather than in your own. Such devotion has great meaning. Just wait and you can be sure that you shall be reborn here. At that time it will be natural and consistent with the will of heaven for you to be entrusted with the highest duties of the land. But by acting as if you were in a hurry you really prove that you're still Westerners."

In the Traditional Language of Politics, Communism Has Seemed More a Fulfillment Than a Break with the Past

In trying to understand why the Communists have been so effective in Viet Nam, one must realize that the Vietnamese, in contrast to the West, do not look upon their society in secular terms. Western civilization separates religion and the state, the spiritual and the temporal; East Asian civilization grasps them as a unity. The Vietnamese don't make distinctions between religion and politics in their thinking about society, because they regard such a process as artificial; the whole of society is what they are betting on. Because of this approach, their history has never developed in an evolutionary way, but has gone spasmodically from catastrophe to catastrophe.

Since they felt that they could not change any one part of society without changing the whole, the potential for evolutionary change among the Vietnamese has been limited indeed. For example, when the West goes along with a rightist faction in Viet Nam and it prevails over its rivals, we should not expect them to be concerned about political and economic issues. To them the very fact that they have prevailed would be an indication that their mode of politics is correct.

On many occasions in Viet Nam, newcomers from France were surprised to realize that they were closer to the Communist Vietnamese than to other local political groups when talking about the nature of society. These Communists spoke the French language of society, even though it was in a Marxist dialect, and, despite obvious differences, their terminology and their logic blended in with that of the West. Consequently, both the French and the orthodox Vietnamese Marxists faced the same problem when they tried to communicate with the mass of the people, who had been trained in traditions as distant from the tenets of Vietnamese Marxism as they were from Western democracy. Above all, the Marxist leaders have had a very hard time dealing with the effect of a cultural and linguistic situation in which modern expressions must first be expressed in Chinese in order to be incorporated into the Vietnamese language. But words chosen from Chinese to express a scientific and political concept are, when introduced into Viet Nam, permeated with local implications that are foreign to China. One can easily sense the consequences of such a shift.

For example, with what kind of rhetoric can a revolutionary platform be best presented to the half-proletarianized *tá diền* (tenant farmers) of the Mekong Delta? "To socialize" and in particular to socialize landed property is expressed as *xã hội hóa*: "to put in common." Social and political coloration is greatly dependent on the first word, *xã*. In it we find the Chinese *she*: "society, commercial company, community"; used with *hui* (in Vietnamese *hội*)—meaning "union, assembly, society"—it corresponds in all its uses to our word "society"; *she-hui-hsüeh,* for example, means "sociology" in Chinese. Together with a word designating a political party, the pair *xã hội* is the usual equivalent of "socialism."

But if we stop here we wouldn't have an idea of all that it conveys. Indeed, *xã* has been used specifically as a designation for the traditional village with all its spiritual and social connotations. In order to understand the linguistic significance here we must go back to the writing of Paul Ory, the French administrator of a province in Tonkin: "The ideographical sign *xã* which designates the village means: spirit of the earth. . . . It is composed of two characters or roots, *thi* and *thổ,* the first meaning everything that refers to spirits and the other expressing the notion of that which is earthly. . . . Both characters together give the idea of a gathering place for individuals sacrificing to the spirits," not to spirits in general, but to the patron spirit of the village, whose altar is expressed by the character *xã* in one of its basic meanings.

From this vocabulary one can see another reason why village life is the most fundamental expression of Vietnamese society. In a fine monograph entitled *Le Culte du genie tutelaire des villages au Tonkin* (*The Cult of the Tutelary Genie in the Villages of Tonkin*), Paul Mus's friend and colleague Nguyen Van Khoan has shown how the whole moral and social structure of a village takes shape around a spiritual cult. The cult sums up the life of the village by expressing that irreducible element of Vietnamese spiritual identity in terms of philosophical formalism borrowed from China. Within such a tradition the modern program of "socialization," when expressed in a familiar idiom, does not give small landowners, either actual or potential ones, the impression of a break with their past. At their level of information and judgment it would appear, on the contrary, to be a new fulfillment of their traditions, which had been weakened by a French regime that had allowed the establishment of large landholdings in violation of customary law.

In the consciousness of the Vietnamese masses the word *xã* has a central value. It unfolds a landscape—not a physical landscape but a sociological landscape. Yet we have observed that the physical landscape of Viet Nam reflects the pattern of the country's society and that within this society the village, or *xã*, comes before all else; one belongs to the village before one belongs to oneself. Anywhere the village does not exist in the country's territory Viet Nam has yet to come into its own against the forests, the Chams, or the Cambodians; the national soil was constituted in exactly this way.

In the Mekong Delta the obstacle to establishing villages along traditional lines was the large landholdings resulting from French colonial policies, which prevented the creation of communal land and the maintenance of local village cults. By observing these cults men acknowledge the spirits of their ancestors as the authentic owners of the land. In a society that knows far better than those in the West do that life is made up more of the dead than the living, rights were thought to come from observing the wishes of one's ancestors. In the Vietnamese mentality, life is merely a brief transit, and the foundation for living remains beneath the mobility of people.

A socialization of the land defined by the words *xã hội hóa* thus suggests not a spurious adventure and the disorder of social innovation, but the traditionally communal values that are most reassuring to the masses. The verb *hóa* completes this Confucian imagery. Far from denoting an anarchic convulsion, it applies specifically to the action in depth by which the "mandate of heaven," through its trustees, the imperial rulers, civilizes a country. This action brings out what man's social nature potentially contains everywhere in Viet Nam: a patriarchal organization at least partially collectivized (remember that in central Viet Nam, a traditional land, 26 percent of the fields were communal property) and based on the ancient model in accordance with the decrees of heaven.

The Peasant's Spiritual Sense About Politics

To understand the impact of Communism on East Asia it is necessary to grasp the fundamental yet antithetic analogy between animist cosmology and Marxist cosmology. For anyone who is inclined to doubt the lasting hold that ancient cosmic spiritualism has over even confirmed Communist militants, we can mention the report drawn up in 1927 by Mao Tse-tung on the state of the agrarian movement in Hunan province in China. Nineteen twenty-seven was a tragic year for Chinese Communism, since it witnessed the massacre of party militants in Shanghai, Nanking, and Peking. Yet Mao, bursting with the success achieved by peasant groups the year before, did not hesitate to write in a manner which ignored the classical doctrine that only the industrial proletariat is pure revolutionary material:

> The force of the peasantry is comparable to that of raging winds or torrential rain. Its violence grows so rapidly, no power would be able to stop it. The peasantry will rip open all the chains that crush it; it will dash down the road to liberation. Beneath it, it will bury all the imperial forces, militarism, the corruption of civil servants, the village notables, and the bad landowners. All the revolutionary parties, all the comrades of the revolutionaries will pass in review before it and be scrutinized and it will accept them or reject them. Shall we take our position as the advanced guard to lead it or shall we stay behind to oppose it?

No one has put more energy or more classical expression into describing peasants as the embodiment of a natural catastrophe, provoked by the "spirit" of the rivers and mountains. Far from being the instigator, Marxism itself is looking for acceptance among distressed peasants. In 1927, of course, Mao had not yet discovered all the elements of his success, especially his style in military organization—an element without which even a Jacquerie finds itself impotent. But in 1927, he was prophetizing more than organizing (his time would come soon), and the torrential flow that he describes within man is the animation of a cosmos.

A similar expression of the spiritual sense of politics among peasants is an oath taken by some Vietnamese political conspirators, a copy of which was found in the archives of the French law courts in Cochin China:

> Come O Gods who walk on the clouds and through the rains! Teach us the power of transfiguring ourselves and of thrusting ourselves upon the forces of the devils and the armies of ghosts. . . . Heaven and earth have very far-reaching powers: we beseech them to grant us the power to stop monsters [the French], the power to attract all creatures to us, to make the wind and the rain. . . .

Thus in 1916, there was an insurrection in Saigon led by the pseudo "Heavenly Emperor" Pham Xich Long, a simple charlatan and fortuneteller in the Cochin Chinese market places. This forerunner of the founders of the politico-religious sects merely called together, in a protest against French rule, some one hundred peasants armed with sabers and even some who were unarmed except for amulets, which they felt had magical power. For them it was clear that they had done their part and the spirits of the raging wind and the torrential rain had to do the rest. In Viet Nam, too, it was Communism that taught the peasants the art of organizing an army on a territorial basis.

These comparisons show in an unexpected way how deeply rooted such ways of thinking and feeling are in East Asia and how they have influenced the processes of revolutionary thought. Of course, this animist cosmos was only a starting point for revolutionaries like Mao Tse-tung. Even in his long march to the north-west, where he was to set out on his conquest of China, we know how carefully Mao kept his group of party faithful in tune with the spirit of the proletariat—in the absence of proletarians. If the old East Asian "cosmological" background remained the framework for the thought of sophisticated Chinese Communist leaders with exposure to Western learning, think how strong it must have been among the masses of the Tonkin Delta, for example. They live according to impulses more than knowledge and to them Western ideas are almost completely foreign (Marxists are seen as Westerners). Such peasant masses are constantly threatened by pauperism without having been organized into a proletariat.

Here we have the basis of the whole analysis of the politics of revolution in Viet Nam. According to sound doctrines of Marxism, the mission of the proletariat is to reconvert industry from an instrument of the exploitation of man by man into an instrument for the exploitation of nature. Such a reconversion was necessary because of a "historically" inevitable process in which the few received an excessive amount of control over the many. But in Viet Nam, industrial capitalism never developed as part of the colonial system. Instead the French imposed a system that permitted usury to develop on the part of a wealthy Vietnamese upper class who were taking advantage of their lower-class brethren. Obviously this situation was inherently unstable, but the presence of the French administrative network gave a deceptive sense of order to the country.

Nonetheless there was no proletariat in Viet Nam prepared for a Marxist mission of any kind. In Tonkin and Annam as well as Cochin China, there was a very dense multitude of small landowners and behind them an agitated strata of candidates for the small parcels of land already occupied. In indoctrinating the peasantry, the only thing that revolutionaries can count on is their attachment to traditional superstitions. Their reactions are not dissimilar to those of the *narodniks* in the Russian countryside, against whom Lenin was doctrinally so vigilant while knowing how to form an alliance with them.

The practical consequences of this are of the greatest significance for a political perspective on Viet Nam. The peasant as an instrument of politics is, by reason of his numbers, the only instrument that counts in Viet Nam. If one goes against the nature of the peasants, they are difficult to manage politically. If heaven seems to question those in power at the time, an insurrection will follow no matter who is on top. There is no final struggle, and the instinctive expectation would be that the accomplishment of the Marxist "paradise," even if one had proof of its finality, must pass like others.

The Peasant Politics of "Wait-and-See"

In response to the world international conflict being fought right now in Viet Nam, we notice that there has taken shape in the minds of the Vietnamese peasants a politics of "wait-and-see," which is essentially a traditionalist formula. The instinctive reaction of the Vietnamese countryside, whenever they aren't sure who is going to win an internal conflict, is not to take any part in the game, not even with the adventurous hope of arbitrating it. From what the peasant can know of the international situation or from what he has seen in his own country through this long, arduous war, it is clear to him that such evasion is not easy. This is why his reaction isn't always rational. His attempts at escape from the war, especially in the critical zones of the Mekong Delta, result in withdrawal whose mythical nature is disclosed precisely by the recourse he seeks in the politico-religious sects, the Hoa Hao and the Cao Dai. These substitute religions, which are pregnant with a whole social plan and which promise a new world, have had a localized success that is revealing.

However, a reticence in facing current facts may be found in varying degrees in many Vietnamese political groups in addition to the politico-religious sects, and sometimes they carry the tendency to the point of schizophrenia. Needless to say, this reticence is mixed with other political components. For example, within the conservative Vietnamese bourgeoisie there will be avowed partisans for a particular cause, but in all of them one perceives from time to time an inkling of that reticence: it puts the brakes on any potentially deep political commitment.

A major source of this disquiet and anxiety among the Vietnamese is the suspicion that they may not have chosen the winning side. Therefore, they feel that it is probably wise for them not to be deeply committed lest they find it too difficult to change sides easily and quickly. In many areas of the country the tide of battle has shifted so frequently that this reticence of wait-and-see has been not only a prudent judgment but also a necessity for survival. Moreover, since the signs of the "virtue" of the competitor regimes in Viet Nam's revolution have been ambiguous, it is understandable that the peasants have tried to avoid choosing sides at all. At the same time, they have used their traditional concepts of politics to measure the prospects of the various revolutionary competitors in demonstrating the "virtue," the complete new system of politics, which is the sign of a new mandate of heaven. And as they have perceived this sign to be more explicit and dependable, the peasants have abandoned their wait-and-see attitude with a speed that is just as surprising to Westerners as is the depth of their newly found commitment.

One of the classic examples of a revolutionary competitor trying to respond to these traditionalist expectations occurred in 1945, when the Indochina Communist Party gave clear evidence of how important it considered the influence of the wait-and-see attitude. In a stunning move it relinquished its name as a Communist Party in favor of a socialistic formula that was more to the local taste, while at the same time it maintained its party structure.

Usually, the Marxist leaders of the Democratic Republic of Viet Nam have heeded the traditional beliefs of the peasants. However, they deliberately diverged from this pattern in 1930 when they chose the name of their party, "The Indochinese Communist Party," which is expressed in Vietnamese as *Đông Dương Cộng Sản Đảng*. Such a title signifies values that are foreign, if not actually opposed, to the traditions of the people. For example, using the phrase *xã hội* to indicate a plan for the redistribution of land evokes institutions which are tempered by customary experience. *Cộng Sản* (Communism), on the contrary, disregards this.

Cộng signifies direct action taken in common which puts bodies and will together physically; there is no longer any question of gathering to sacrifice to the spirits. It connotes another social landscape. *Sản* is a word rich in meaning; its sense as "product, profit, income " covers the modern industrial aspect of the Marxist takeover, but it also means "patrimony." Applied to the horizon of a Vietnamese village we thus get a glimpse in the words *cộng sản* of a complete takeover by the direct cultivators from the local capitalists.

But what will be the nature of the collectivization implied in the word *cộng*? This word eliminates the traditional social groups in their religious structure by condemning them as an idealistic and parasitic superstructure. But what meaning can such ideas have today for the Vietnamese peasants at this stage of their mental development? *Xã hội* sees the future of Viet Nam as being dependent on its past and on a tradition which predates the French occupation. Over and above this occupation, a liberated Viet Nam would coincide with all the potential of its past that is adaptable to the world today. *Cộng sản,* on the contrary, would maintain and augment the characteristics of secularization, which is the dominant feature of the Western colonial era. From the perspective of Vietnamese nationalism, secularity is not merely an antireligious position in the European sense of the term; it is the complete loss of the religious feeling about the state. Carried to their logical conclusion, these two formulas of Vietnamese Communism, *cộng sản* and *xã hội,* set up a radical contradiction within the party's political strategy.

By its very nature Marxism acknowledges a direct bond of kinship with the society that precedes it. In Viet Nam the kinship between Marxism and French colonialism was one of opposition or, rather, inversion. For a third party on the other hand—and certain Vietnamese nationalists took that position—it may appear that between Marxism and the French there was a similarity in species. Despite the direct conflict between Marxism and colonialism or perhaps because of it, Marxism deals with economic, technical, and political problems that the French introduced in Viet Nam. To do this, it uses the French vocabulary and is often stuck when it must find equivalents in the Vietnamese language.

Without the Europeans apparently even noticing, the name of the Indochina Communist Party expressed, paradoxically, an imperialist and Communist ideal. In 1945, while the traditional name of the country, Viet Nam, was hailed everywhere as the promise of a new future as an independent nation, the name of the Indochina Communist Party, *Đông Dương Cộng Sản Đảng,* bore the name of Indochina, which was a creation of French colonialism from disparate traditional states along the Mekong River that were organized into the kingdoms of Laos and Cambodia. In East Asia words are facts and they direct those facts, and in the Vietnamese cosmology they produce reactions that can be easily determined. *Đông Dương,* a Vietnamese expression that normally signified the word Indochina, means etymologically: "Country of the Great Eastern Sea," and more specifically Paul Reynaud's phrase "Balcony over the Pacific," which the French used to indicate that Indochina was an extension of their metropolitan house.

But the French house is far away, and to the minds of the Vietnamese that observation is of the greatest significance. They considered "Indochina" on their silver coins, on their bank notes, on their stamps, and on the French stationery as a sign of bondage. How else could they have understood the implication of two words in their language which far from giving their country a geographic independence served to relegate them to a distant sea at the end of the world in the "Far East," by determining its location in relation to the West? Doubtless the historic name *Việt Nam* (Nam means south in Vietnamese) situated them to the south of China, but it included a proper name—*Việt*—that was felt to be national. It reintegrated them into the Asia to which they belonged; there it was understood that China belonged in the middle.

In dropping its name the Indochina Communist Party sought to reassure traditionalist sentiment, which was inclined to see Communism as a devilry left behind by the occupation of Westerners. Give and take: we must understand that the temporary elimination of the party's terminology at the moment of its great triumph in 1945 was not as small or even as deceitful a sacrifice as we might think. Of course, we realized that the masses traditionally consider the competition of candidates, organized groups, or peoples as a game of destiny. This explains the importance attached to the fact that while the game is being played out, a person can easily withdraw his bet.

Since the stakes of the game are the people's adherence to a doctrine, everything must be started over again from scratch and thus the long way around must be taken. Under the circumstances this meant that the Communists had to institute a moderate program of socialization to reassure the peasants. They achieved this by making rules against any interference with the rights of property, drawing up a constitution which, for the French, was unexpectedly moderate, and, finally, having representatives of the old order of things in the provincial councils or in the government. Of course, the Communists took care to keep the key posts in the government assigned to their staunchest adherents.

It is easy to say that in 1945 the Communists were dropping the shadow for the substance. But this view overlooks how essential and how definitive the Indochina Communist Party was for the Vietnamese popular imagination. In the historic light in which the Democratic Republic of Viet Nam was launched by the August Revolution of 1945, the Communist Party was little known except for its revolutionary victory. In effect, the party was renouncing its immediate rights over the masses by giving up its name. According to a rule of the game—a game it had no more control over than the French did—it realized that while having been a factor in its emergence, the word of heaven did not yet point specifically to the Communist Party. At the very most the party was commending itself to a future opportunity to receive the mandate of heaven.

Such comments are in no way a disguised apologia for the party and should not be taken as a rationalization. Indeed, this explanation contains some bitter truths which the French did not comprehend. In view of Vietnamese public opinion—which, although it often eluded the French, exists nonetheless and is sovereign in its own way—Ho Chi Minh through his politics during that critical period from August, 1945, to March, 1946, secured a strong bond between the non-Marxist nationalists and the Communist Party by withdrawing doctrinally. Instead of staking everything on the "trick" by which he had won power through a *coup d'état* in August, 1945, Ho decided to make a change. He thus held his own against all comers, avoiding any clashes and allowing "heaven" —in other words, the situation at hand—to be disposed in his favor.

8.

The Marxist World View and Revolutions in Modernizing Countries

What meaning can militant Marxism—fashioned as it is on the complexities of life in the Western world—have for Vietnamese villagers whose life is so elementary? The answer is simple. In the 1940's and 1950's as well as today, Marxism had meaning only to the extent that it was known to be associated with the nationalist movement against foreign rule. If there were any subtle distinctions to be made about Marxism as a political ideology, they were left to the theorists. This was the case because Viet Nam in the 1940's, when revolution occurred, was not perceptibly affected by the Marxist dichotomy between a proletariat "deprived of property" and a "propertied" bourgeoisie.

While a wealthy class had emerged, mostly from moneylending, it was not very large. And in a country covered with very small landowners, demographic problems had cropped up, but—except for the Mekong Delta—proletarianization had not yet come about. Therefore, the terminology of doctrinaire Marxist propaganda has had little meaning for the villagers even though it has been spread all the way to the countryside. But despite its doctrinal meaninglessness, the villagers regarded this propaganda as a signal for rallying against French military forces and colonial institutions. In the tradition of peasant revolts these villagers rose up because they believed they had seen the sign of a broad uprising and not because of any particular response to Marxist ideology.

In contrast to this explanation, one might have been inclined to see an indication of an acceptance of Marxist orthodoxy in the persistent naming of the Bank of Indochina, that convenient symbol of French colonialism, as the chief enemy to be overthrown by the Vietnamese. The fact that the slogan was spread to remote villages would seem to testify to the success of such propaganda. But in reality the peasant had very little precise knowledge about the French. At his level, the peasant mostly met the Vietnamese who worked with the French administration, not French officials themselves. He had even less knowledge of colonial institutions, which he didn't fully understand. The Bank of Indochina, however, was known everywhere by its paper currency since this visible substance of the wealth of the country came from the bank's coffers and went back to them; on its bills were the signatures of its directors, who were known as foreigners. Such a situation seemed unreasonable to the common people who were educated enough to feel that a country ought, in the first instance, to have its own money. This was a national claim and had no real connection with the more sophisticated formulas of the class struggle.

Since a capitalist economy has existed only within enclaves in their countries, capitalism has not been completely understood by colonial and postcolonial peoples. And because so few of them had been a part of this alien economy or shared its rewards, they opposed it. But their opposition was a nationalistic one and not a class antagonism, because class distinctions among the approximately three-fourths of the people who are peasants have been slight and, overall, less important than considerations of a national political identity in motivating revolutionary commitment. Consequently, when revolution broke out in Viet Nam in 1945, it was a nationalist manifestation. Yet, from the very beginning the Communist Party stood at the center of the coalition that was seeking independence through revolution. Many observers regarded this Communist presence as a Trojan Horse. But weren't these Communists simply using nationalism as a pretext for overthrowing French rule so that they might then eliminate their Vietnamese adversaries and achieve total control over the country? Was the revolution begun in 1945 a genuine nationalist movement or was it merely a Communist plot?

The Marxist Strategy of Revolution

These questions are too important to risk giving an emotional answer. First, one must acknowledge that Marxists will often co-operate with other revolutionaries if it serves their own purposes. Of course, it is a very natural defensive reaction to see such a tactic as an example of Marxist treachery. Yet this reaction may obscure an underlying element of the situation which is bound up with the Communist methods we are trying to discern. For our own benefit it is necessary to examine more closely and dispassionately the attitude of Marxist leaders in modernizing countries with regard to their nationalist allies. In doing so one must keep in mind the local "revolutionary" circumstances which are so foreign to the economic and political framework of social revolution in the West.

Because of local circumstances the Asian Marxists—when they unite with antitraditionalist or anticolonialist nationalists—are not, as we have thought, so sure that their temporary allies are wrong. On the contrary, the educated militant Marxists believe that the nationalists are right at their own level—that they are even righter than they think. What characterizes the authentic Marxist is not only that he knows the mistakes of his allies and therefore prepares to do away with them as soon as possible, but also that he knows their truth and what they represent better than they do. For this reason the Asian Marxist considers himself called upon to go beyond his nationalist allies; he feels he must take charge of their revolutionary movement because they do not recognize what is valid in it.

This distinction may seem too subtle for non-Marxists, but for Marxists such distinctions between phases of revolution are essential. These distinctions are especially relevant to revolution in modernizing societies, since their level of development is so different from the conditions on which Marxist theories were orig-inally focused. In circumstances where class antagonisms are a less significant source of political discontent, Marxists must relate their doctrines to the revolutionary situation as it actually exists or else their influence over the course of a revolution promises to be minimal indeed. But by acknowledging that revolutions in modernizing societies must initially go through a "nationalist" phase, in which there is a consolidation of national leadership by the elimination of colonial rule or archaic traditionalist rule, the Marxists anticipate succeeding revolutionary phases in which far-reaching social change can, indeed must, be brought about. Here the Marxists reap their doctrinal advantage, since those who are struggling with only the "nationalist" phase in mind tend not to realize the full dimensions nor, therefore, the total requirements for revolutionary change.

These Marxist distinctions about phases of revolution may seem purely arbitrary or even artificial; they might appear to be designed only for subverting Marxist competitors rather than assessing the underlying nature of a revolutionary situation. Such an appearance of artificiality, however, could only arise when one thinks in discursive patterns of thought—that is, patterns that are linked by analogies. But in dialectic thought—that is, patterns of thought which develop by "overcoming," or coming to grips with, contradictions and reconciling them—there is no artificiality about these phases of revolution and the action required to achieve them. To quote Hegel, from whom Marx borrowed the principle, "Woe unto anyone who cannot deal with contradictions!" Ignoring or denouncing the strangeness of this Marxist pattern of thought is not enough. If one is to understand the revolutionary action that springs from this Marxist method of thought, one must follow it to its roots.

Marxists do not sit around constructing an imaginary "future city" the way socialists do. Marxism believes that its ideal must emerge from the existing state of human society. Such is the "contradiction" that it has to overcome in order to exist. Such is the servitude of Marxism with regard to the society it destroys. It must come to grips with the reality of that society in order to move out of it. We have not always realized just how unimaginative and undiscursive the militant doctrine of Marxism is meant to be. What we in the West build up with imagination and discursive logic the Marxists consider mere superstructure. The real society, they believe, emerges only from a real foundation. In other words, it emerges from the authentic previous conditions.

Historians have observed that Karl Marx refrained from describing "Marxist" society; any attempt at that would have been a repudiation of all that he was trying to achieve. What he provided was the principle that creates the "Marxist" society. Using his imagination would have meant a lapse into ideological vanity. And such a vanity thinks only in terms of superstructures and does not create norms for the future. The task lay elsewhere. Its ground is action. "Force is the midwife of any society in labor." Thus one doesn't get lost in utopias.

In the West, where the Marxist concept of revolution was first formulated, it was originally meant to be a subversion of the nationalist revolution from within—a *genetic* subversion. The Marxist revolutionary strategy was to take over the leadership of the "nationalist" phase by insinuating its cadre into the economic, political, and then the military structure of a highly industrialized society—the type of society that Marxism usually identifies as its point of departure. Through its pattern of development, industrial capitalism made revolution a possibility in certain European countries by provoking a gradual dehumanization (*Entmenschung*) of its workers and turning them into an indigent, unpropertied class, or proletariat, which had virtually none of the rewards from the economic system its labor was building. In this way industrial capitalism became "its own gravedigger" because it prepared the way for its own potential destruction. From the Marxist viewpoint, the remedy for this situation was a revolution that would result in the complete transfer to the proletariat of control over the total means of industrial production in a society. Through this dialectic of revolution, the proletariat would receive the industrial enterprises which their labor was responsible for constructing and operating, but in whose output they had not shared.

From these dialectics we can see how Marxism conceives the historical process of revolution. In Marxist strategy a revolution is not supposed to destroy the previous condition of society but, instead, to actualize it and consequently to realize its social potential. By destroying the capitalist system all that would be removed by the Marxists is the scaffolding, which was useful in its time and had served to build the structure. But the structure itself would not be touched. Such is dialectical materialism as applied to human societies. Following this dialectic, a prerevolutionary situation would be one in which the structure of society is ready to be taken over by those whom it has ignored.

Yet it takes a good eye to be able to choose the right moment. Any revolution that's not based on the profound discontent of the mass of the population may merely result in an abortive insurrection. Given the circumstances in nineteenth-century Europe, for example, revolutions could only be unsuccessful bourgeoise uprisings; only the middle classes had experienced such a widespread frustration that they were anxious and capable of attempts at overthrowing oppressive regimes. But whatever hopes these uprisings aroused among the lower classes, the abortive revolutions of the nineteenth century could not have led, from the Marxist point of view, to an "authentic" proletarian revolution—that is, a revolution that gave control over society to those who had previously been dispossessed by it.

After his fleeting enthusiasm for the revolutions of 1848, Marx had to temper his optimism greatly concerning the "inevitable" and "genetic" nature of the expropriation of the capitalist expropriators. Since then history has not produced a new—and final—social order from the economic antecedents that *Das Kapital* had prescribed for it. Everywhere that a proletarian revolution began to take shape it was broken up, with the exception of October 1917, a date of primary importance in the history of Marxism.

It is easy, of course, to point out that this successful enterprise in Russia did not come as an exemplary illustration of the Marxist dialectic but took place in the least industrialized country of Europe and only after that country had been exhausted by its participation in World War I. But more to the point is the fact that the Bolsheviks triumphed in Russia because Lenin in a realistic spirit—since he refused to be inactive while awaiting some kind of Marxist millennium—had deeply politicized the perspectives and methods of revolution. Lenin's strategy was no longer Marxism in the strict economic sense: it was forcing and accelerating a process which

Marx felt would occur inevitably. If one prefers the kind of images that Karl Marx was fond of, Lenin's strategy saw revolution as a Caesarean birth.

The Relevance of Marxist Revolutionary Strategy to Asian Societies

What about such perspectives when transposed to Asia and particularly to Viet Nam? Since a question of this sort can easily be misinterpreted, an answer must be sought in a broad setting. First, we must recognize that colonial economies such as the one in Viet Nam were not capitalist economies. Capitalism was never established in colonies except as small enclaves whose effect was to produce societies which did not conform to the Marxist view of the proletarianization of the population. Here we discover both the strength and the servitude of Marxism with regard to the antecedents it imposes upon itself. Dialectic materialism puts Marxism under the obligation of preserving the world from which it must emerge. A Marxist revolution merely means changing the distribution of rewards within a pre-existing world. The rewards will be taken from the parasitic "leaders"—those captains of the superstructure of society—and given to the producers, who constitute the infrastructure. The latter are more than the salt of the earth; they are the world itself, because in Marxist terms "all value is but crystallized human labor."

In the struggle between Marxism and capitalism it is inevitable that the adversaries will take every opportunity to borrow something from what they are opposing. Each one is in part what the other makes of it. Now in Southeast Asia where the dialectic of Marxism is vying with the West, that dialectic cannot help but be hindered by the fact that capitalism did not build itself up there but used the colonialized domain indirectly as a support and no more. There, Marxist revolution does not find the central structures of capitalism as in Europe or the United States, but merely outposts and extensions of capitalism.

Therefore, revolution in such colonial locations cannot be

thought of as the veritable proletarian revolution. Any other perspective would be purely ideological and, in the last analysis, a Marxist deviation. Wherever capitalism has not yet installed the instruments of its full realization—a monopoly control over the means of production—rebellions, whether justified or unjustified, successful or unsuccessful, may arise or be provoked, but they must not be mistaken for a proletarian revolution. Anticolonial revolutions when reduced to what they truly signify have nothing to do with a proletarian revolution. Inherent in the Marxist strategy of revolution is the fact that a nationalist revolution in a country without a prominent industrial background does not furnish the Marxists with any more valid antecedent than did the colonial society itself.

However, this nationalist revolution may serve as an intermediate phase and allow time to prepare a field of action for the future. In the interim, economic and social developments may be capable of creating an authentic prerevolutionary situation—one which is able to give Marxism the opportunity of springing forth. The realization of Marxism is never a matter of theory; it is a matter of fact. And given its basic concept of historical materialism, Marxism cannot be imagined as originating on a blank page or in a test tube; it must be heavy with living economic substance, pregnant with it alone, and prepared for birth by a dialectic whose laws, the Marxists believe, are inevitably followed by capitalism.

Because of the nature of Marxism there will be struggles between it and capitalism in the modernizing world; they are the two cosmic rivals of our time. Just as in earlier centuries the struggle to acquire colonial empires added another dimension of conflict between European nations, so too will the capitalist world and the Marxist world enter into a test of strength in peripheral areas. In carrying out this struggle, tactics that are suitable to a particular place and to nowhere else will again have to be invented by both sides. Because of this need for flexibility, both capitalism and Marxism will adopt policies that seem uncharacteristic. Let us take Indochina as a direct example and let us look at it from the perspective of European history.

Mass Mobilization as a Technique of Revolution

During the nineteenth century the evolution of the economic, demographic, political, and technical structure of Europe led its nations to regard general mobilization as an indispensable preparation for the conduct of war. Gradually, the development of industrial production had become adequate to support mass warfare. Obviously, an industrial economy could now more easily become a war economy, making it possible for a preponderant number of able-bodied men, trained in the use of weapons, to be diverted from their normal activities to devote themselves to external imperialist conquest or to defend against it. The new techniques of stockpiling and the new means of transportation were also instrumental in making total war possible. In this new type of war men, who had to be shifted between battlefields by tens and hundreds of thousands, became a new kind of matériel that had to be conditioned, supplied, retrieved, reconditioned, and redistributed. After more than a century of existence this landscape of total war has become quite familiar to us.

When the process of general mobilization is adopted for purely economic purposes, apart from supporting a national military effort, it becomes more intense. Yet, in this economic context the phrase "general mobilization" is quite fitting. For in a given situation the productive elements which are required are ones that have been pulled out of fixed circumstances and put at the disposal of others; these needed resources have been "mobilized." Everything in the history of the development of industrial techniques shows that tools and methods invented for some particular purpose may, once they exist, serve other purposes. Thus the rules for the military discipline of massive numbers, which protected an armed nation against desertion, were used again in another kind of conflict: a mobilization against strikes which used military sanctions against the workers in order to ensure all the necessary services for an industrial society. Here was a technique quite as foreign to the seventeenth and early eighteenth centuries as the idea of an armed nation, just as it was a precursor of the totalitarian societies of the twentieth.

Against this scheme of political order through paramilitary mobilization and discipline, the key revolutionary tactic is as clear in its conception as it is beset with difficulties. No doubt the worst problem for the revolutionaries lies in establishing an organization which can evade and eventually destroy the disciplined political mobilization of the incumbents. Infiltration, scattered strikes, a general strike, and insurrection are steps to the conquest of power; yet, such a revolutionary war tries to undercut the political mobilization of a nation through efforts to deny popular compliance with the will of the incumbent regime. In order to do that the revolutionaries destroy the legal and moral ties which attach men to a prevailing system and then they unite their new adherents against that system through passive action and, if need be, fighting in the streets and countryside until a revolutionary government has achieved a predominance of power. After its victory the new regime integrates the revolutionary coalition into a new system with binding legal and moral ties, a system which it hopes to discipline through political mobilization in much the same manner as the regime it has overthrown.

Here in revolutionary war, just as in war between nations, nothing is obtained without an adequate effect of massive numbers. Daring men and good technicians are indispensable to preparing the way and, in recognizing this, Lenin greatly added to the views of Karl Marx, who was essentially an armchair philosopher. But in an authentic revolutionary situation it must, above all, be the people—that giant in chains—who shake off their fetters. What fetters? That is the whole point of Marxism! For Marxism, the nature of the exploitation predetermines the character of revolution. Thus it is capitalism that mobilizes not only its own forces but also those of the proletarian revolution. In essence the proletrian revolution is not a creation but an inversion of forms brought into being by its predecessors; in absolute values it has the same substance as the previous state.

In modernizing societies where there is no chance for an authentic proletarian revolution, Marxists also rely on the techniques of mass mobilization as a means of asserting their leadership. However, during the initial, "nationalist" phase of revolutionary

conflict, Marxists will not have, as they do in highly industrialized societies, a population which has been extensively mobilized
for economic purposes. Indeed, only in the small enclaves where
the capitalist system has been imposed in colonial and traditionalist societies will there be a mobile population that can be brought
into revolutionary action very easily. But these enclaves are also
the areas most easily controlled by the forces of the incumbent
regimes, and therefore the countryside of modernizing societies
becomes a crucial focus for revolutionary activity. It is here that
the Marxists have been able to adapt their alien doctrine to the traditionalist concepts of society in Viet Nam, and through their total
scheme for the political life of the country they have shown the
sign of a new "virtue," which the peasants have seen as a signal
for an uprising in response to a new mandate of heaven.

The cosmology of Marxism has, therefore, influenced revolution in Viet Nam, as well as in other modernizing societies, in two
important ways. Through its adaptation to the traditional cosmology of the Vietnamese peasants the Marxist cosmology has laid
the basis for a political community in which village people have
found—in an idiom familiar to them—a new rationalization for
participation in national politics. Not only have they risen up in
response to a sign of a new mandate of heaven, but these villagers
have, in the process, also become participants in a revolutionary
movement which offers them a means of sharing in national political power and in gaining access to the attributes of modern life.
How could a peasant be an effective revolutionary if he could not
read or write, and how could he be expected to be an aggressive
revolutionary if he did not believe that his energies would result
in a change in the pattern of authority and the sharing of rewards
from politics? The answer is that as the peasant followed the lead
of the Communists in rising up against colonial rule, he also drew
closer to the modern world and to a national political identity.

Closely related to these modernizing influences of the cosmology of Marxism has been an operational, or strategic, influence.
The total assessment the cosmology makes of the underlying
nature of the revolutionary process has led Marxist leaders to
look beyond the "nationalist" phase of revolution. With this

perspective they have realized that the replacement of colonial or traditionalist rule by a cohesive nationalist leadership is not an ultimate goal but merely an initial step. Consequently, Marxists believe that revolutionary change requires the total participation of a people and not just the raising of a force powerful enough to overthrow an incumbent regime. By acting on this perception, the Marxists went beyond their competitors in preparing to mobilize the Vietnamese for revolution, a preparation which catapulted them into the vanguard of revolutionary leadership as the most vocal and effective advocates of Vietnamese nationalism.

Any contradiction between their commitment to Marxism and their championing of Vietnamese nationalism was apparent only in the eyes of their adversaries and not in the minds of this Marxist revolutionary leadership. Quite the contrary, it was precisely because of their cosmology of Marxism, with its total assessment and awareness of revolution, that the Marxists were able to outperform their nationalist competitors and take charge of the revolutionary movement in Viet Nam. Their effectiveness was not so much a result of the insidiousness of Marxism as it was attributable to the comprehensiveness of their strategy of revolution. And if the revolution begun in 1945 in Viet Nam really has been a Communist plot, it has succeeded more from its profound understanding of revolutionary politics than from its ruthless execution.

9.

The Possibilities for Modernization in Viet Nam

No issue is clear to the Vietnamese mind unless a comprehensive assessment has been made of it. This requires taking the whole situation into consideration and evaluating each part of the problem in terms of its relationship to the whole. Such a way of reasoning is what we have tried to describe and explain in this study: it is a style of thought in which the Vietnamese have shown far more of a feeling for totalities than we in the West have; they aim at the whole and base their thinking and action on it. Let us not forget that over the centuries their minds were formed in Chinese fashion and for the Chinese everything is bound up, through reason or behavior, to a compactness and rigor that Westerners understand only in the most mathematical theories of science. For them the merest event becomes a sign of some larger significance. Consequently, we must realize the degree to which they see our analytical style as simply an effort to put together pieces of a jigsaw puzzle. When we ask them to submit to logical reasoning as we do, such logic in their view merely means fitting two pieces af a puzzle together, whereas they believe everything should be seen as part of the complete image. Such being the case, Western objectivity and progressive methods seem like political expediency to them.

The Village Must Be the Focus of Plans for Modernization

Our whole analysis in this study has been founded on the basic element of Vietnamese social structure: the village. Our major point has been that the village's traditional equilibrium, which had tended to make the Vietnamese secure in their rights and duties, was unable to withstand the impact of French colonial policies. The most significant of these policies was the introduction of money taxes, which demolished the traditional system that was based on an economy of consumption and short-range barter. Significantly, a pamphlet that introduced the young Ho Chi Minh under his early pseudonym, Nguyen Ai Quoc, entitled *Procès de la colonisation française (French Colonialism on Trial)*, contained a harsh denunciation of the sudden and crushing manner which the French used to raise taxes in Viet Nam. A broader study of the question does not show this denunciation to be unfounded, but it does give a different perspective on the problem and allows us to view it as a question of modernization rather than simply posing it as an issue of colonialism versus Communism.

The taxes levied were probably not excessive in proportion to the demands placed on a modern economy; they were indicative of the needs of a state in which the big general departments—public works, communications, education, woods and forests, health, etc.—had become public organizations that required governmental financing. No longer could the village support such pub lic services by providing its own local resources, including *corvées,* to carry out the plans drafted by the central administration; the technology of public works had become too complex and too expensive for peasant villagers. But despite these problems the real objection to such a system is that it did not put enough coined money at the disposal of the peasants who were being asked to become taxpayers. Since the problem still exists long after the departure of France from Viet Nam, the solution is not to reduce taxes but to end the dual economic system in which demands are conceived in the modern sector of the economy and satisfied in the peasant sector.

Did France deliberately demolish the traditional equilibrium of the Vietnamese village in order to ensure its assimilation into the colonial political system and to facilitate tax collection? Looking at the actual texts of French policies we realize that the main preoccupation of colonial administrators was social order rather than economic or merely administrative order. Not surprisingly there was a battle between the partisans in the French colonial administration of the established order who stressed the arguments of stability and security inherent in the traditional system and, on the other hand, the French magistrates, who could not accept the exorbitant powers accorded by customary law to the Council of Notables in the villages.

These magistrates felt strongly that the right of arrest and imprisonment and the right of imposing fines and inflicting corporal punishment without any preliminary investigation, without trial, through a mere ruling, were procedures in violation of the most elementary processes of French concepts of law or of any concepts of justice concerned with human dignity. Nothing ruined the traditional village system more than the dogged action of those jurists. In vain did the civil administrators on policy committees try to explain that the jurists were taking all the prestige and means of action away from the traditional village councils, while they were at the same time asking them to impose entirely new demands such as money taxation.

Since the arguments of the French civil administrators were ignored, we can now see what effect the resulting policies had. "It became more and more obvious," wrote the administrator P. Kresser, in his monograph *La commune Annamite en Cochinchine, le recrutement des Notables,* "that the rich families and intellectuals were losing interest in the affairs of the village. This regrettable state of affairs was due less to indifference than to the decrees of the French administration." On the other hand, one no longer saw the villagers overwhelmed by fines or imprisoned in the village jail because of their lack of respect for a Notable.

Surprisingly the conservative Vietnamese claimed in 1946 that the French civil administrators were right in their concern for traditional village institutions. Despite the changes of several decades, these conservatives were adamant in their belief that traditional institutions could be revived after World War II, and in this extreme position they were unrealistic. "Give us sporting guns," one of the conservatives told us, "and we will lay down the law in our villages. We know whom to deal with." This was said in 1946! Such comments merely show that any plans for rational reconstruction of Viet Nam's society in 1946 would have brought France closer to a certain number of its adversaries than to its Vietnamese allies.

While France's allies credited colonial administrators with an understanding of traditionalist social forces, they were showing their understanding of the economic conditions France had introduced into Viet Nam. They did not appreciate how hard it was for the Vietnamese peasant to earn cash from his traditional agriculture. With the most praiseworthy of human intentions France's representatives as well as its local allies approached Vietnamese society from a point of view that was more ideological than economic.

Integrating Peasants into a Modern Economy

The most important problem facing Viet Nam concerns its economic substructure, where the great body of the population of the country, the peasant villagers, will have to be integrated into a modern economy. Some upper-class Vietnamese, however, reject the thought of modernizing the whole society and instead advocate the return to traditional ways. Such a re-emphasis of traditional society and economy would inevitably result in an urban administrative and capitalist world being grafted onto the Confucian countryside, which would be expected to furnish products and labor to sustain the superstructure of urban society. "But if the countryside is happy that way, as it was in the past, where's the harm in it?" is the answer of conservative nationalism. This objection should not be brushed aside too complacently, for there is much truth in its portrayal of a state of happiness in which the conscience of the village—embodied in the notables and morally determined by everyone—was once a veritable guarantee of social harmony.

An examination of the evidence supports the opinion of many experienced French administrators who believe that traditional village justice was often fair, expert, and more suitable than any judicial administration imposed from the outside. This does not mean that in individual cases there were no arbitrary decisions:

unjust sentences could be very heavy. Yet the results of village justice were closer to equity than that which urban institutions of justice have imposed on the countryside during the colonial era and after. This is a fact but an outdated one, since village institutions have been vitiated.

Without exception everything regarding the administration of justice once took place *in camera* among the people themselves; and as far as they knew, it would go on that way forever. Each judgment committed the village judge, and there was no margin between the community and himself: the society he belonged to had a profound sense of community, and it is this village society which a century of French occupation has gutted. There are now urban concentrations everywhere; the big landowners have disappeared from the villages and have left everything in the hands of managers; the important families are in the cities or possess dwellings there. The local equilibrium and sense of community is lost and nothing will restore it.

The real problem of the countryside concerns not only justice and a sense of community but also education. Yet Paul Mus once heard a consultant from the United Nations advocate the need for modernizing agricultural equipment as a means of increasing production. "In Indochina as elsewhere, a man who has a bulldozer at work no longer wants to plow the land with his hands alone," he said. In certain upland areas equipment might indeed play a useful role, but there seems little use for such machinery in the deltas, where rice is grown. Producing rice in flooded fields is an old technique which, according to Pierre Gourou, is almost perfect at its own level; yet it borders on being horticulture—that is, handiwork. A judicious method of using fertilizer would probably be worth more attention than it has been given, but the most important requirement for the countryside is social and mental equipment.

Moreover, heavy equipment implies concentration of resources. We must ask, Who will reap the profits of such an enterprise? The mutation that must be wrought in the peasantry does not depend on heavy equipment anyway, but is possible only by providing the country people with a social framework that will help them hold out against their own atavism and the traditions of their milieu. Such an adaptation is not feasible either individually or through the mediation of renovated Confucian institutions; it can be brought about only by integrating him into a decentralized program of agricultural and light industrial cooperatives involving both consumers and producers. His traditional community structure predisposes him to this not only through the intrinsic merit of such a program, but also through the value of his former civic training.

In describing Vietnamese society during the last years of French rule, Pierre Gourou strongly emphasized the sense of community that pervaded the lives of the people in the countryside:

> In the Tonkinese [northern] villages the inhabitants get together and form district associations, associations for intellectuals or for military mandarins, clubs for the aged, for wrestlers, singers, for tradesmen, for fans of cockfighting, for whistling-bird breeders, for students of a particular professor. There are even associations made up of people born the same year! Each of these associations has its meetings and banquets and to cover their expenses many of them use the income from landed property that was either a gift or that was bought. Such villages hide a strenuous social life behind a mediocre exterior; the peasants find thousands of opportunities to talk, to discuss, to scheme, to manage their common business and to lead the busy life of men burdened with social obligations.

Such was the real civic training of traditional Viet Nam. This perspective from the description of Gourou shows rather well that the Vietnamese peasant's sense of patriotism and civic competence goes far beyond his concern for his bowl of rice despite superficial opinions to the contrary. "This club spirit," concludes Pierre Gourou, "proves, on the other hand, that in Viet Nam conditions are favorable to cooperative associations. If they are organized in conformity with village traditions they will provide a good solution to the difficulties created by the recent introduction of a monetary economy in the rural areas."

Setting up a new economic system in the Vietnamese countryside is not so easy as one might imagine. Essential to such an undertaking would be to have in hand an economic network of both production and consumption. But in the first place one must eliminate the heretofore inhibiting influence of economic intermediaries, the Chinese moneylenders and rice merchants, who have had a powerful organization for monopolizing the fruits of peasant agriculture. Second, one comes up against the problem of choosing and controlling the elements of management in which there have been some previous endeavors to solve the managerial problem by recruiting personnel from the cities and even from among the Europeans. Just the reverse policy should be adopted in order to recruit people from the countryside for the tasks of a modern agricultural economy. Economic cooperatives should deal with self-conscious units that, within their limited scope, profit by the solidarity described by Pierre Gourou and are capable of developing leadership from within their own ranks.

A broad policy of economic and social reconstruction is needed in order to bring the Vietnamese peasantry into the modern world. The decentralization of industrial production by creating small factories in provincial areas is but one of the necessary conditions for bringing the village into line with a modern economy. Grouped together in industrial cooperatives, the peasant-workers would also become consumers and would, therefore, enter into a monetary economy. The differential profit which is now going into the hands of the Chinese middleman would be eliminated by closing the gap between the urban economy and the village one. But unless the small profits acquired by the projected peasant cooperatives are channeled into capital formation they may fall back into such traditional uses as usurious loans, which inevitably result, through foreclosure, in the accumulation of landed property and the expropriation of small cultivators. Moreover, the breaking of such a tenacious cycle of traditional usury requires means that are not foreign but actually are in harmony with the ethos of the countryside.

It would be unthinkable, and probably impossible, to crush or subdue the local financial initiative of the village, which is flexible, hard to grasp, and adapted to the borrower's mentality. When funds are on the spot and ready to adapt to the farming calendar, they will be sought even if they are offered on usurious terms. In order to alleviate this situation, one might undertake some education aimed at forming a borrowers cooperative through teaching peasants how to keep financial accounts. But the really constructive economic target is the unexpended balances in private or collective budgets, which are the starting point of usurious loans.

Instead of making usurious loans or disbursing these budgetary balances to individuals, a credit cooperative could become an investment institution which might focus its attention on developing the small and even middle-sized Vietnamese enterprises that still remain family ventures for the most part. Modern financing through stocks, making mutual participation possible by a number of credit institutions, should also be established in its simplest form. There also would seem to be room in this realm for financial action that would focus on the construction of basic systems of production rather than on financial speculation—in other words, a social-service bank.

A bank—nationalized if necessary—that would undertake this game of reason and caution should be equipped with agents who would make themselves acquainted with local situations. They would find and back up the families most likely to increase the productivity of their property and who would avoid the triple temptation of usury, vanity, and gambling. The chief purpose of a social-service bank would be to look for other means of stimulating the financial elasticity for assets of the country that would result in the acquisition of modern means of production.

Bringing the peasant into the world cycle through such a process of economic education is a means of providing a social foundation that can be profoundly democratic. In order to complement this social action with economic initiatives, a group of state monopolies should be organized to ensure the country against any intrusion of foreign capital, which might result in external pressure on vital areas of the national economy. In addition, such monopolies would have an educational value in training a local cadre of technicians so that once the Vietnamese had become more extensively familiar with heavy machinery and the technical requirements of modernization, the country would be in a position to welcome and satisfy the needs of foreign investment capital.

Many other plans like these are no doubt just as valid, but from this simple outline based on previous sociological analyses one fact is evident: no modernization of Viet Nam will be effective if the social sciences and technology are not given equal consideration.

Paradoxically, this program of economic and social development parallels closely the program openly demanded by the Communist-led Democratic Republic of Viet Nam. A maturation of *xã hội hóa*, or socialism, integrated into the history of the country is a direct contrast to both the sclerosis of conservatism and to the social formula of Marxism. And in demanding their own brand of socialism the Vietnamese Communists are not merely erecting a façade, they are expressing their recognition of the situation in Viet Nam for what it really is. Without continuity to the country's traditional ethos, a program for the future can produce few practical results. But one may still ask why it is necessary to form such theoretical linkages when the divisions in Vietnamese society are so deep-seated? And another equally difficult question arises; is it possible to build a modern society in Viet Nam as long as the country is not unified and is being torn more jaggedly by war?

The Political Requirements for Modernization

During the First Indochina War 1947-1954, the Prime Minister of the Vietnamese government allied with the French, Mr. Tran Van Huu, raised an intriguing question. He said that if he could assure his country full status of equality among the nations of the world, his countrymen would be so satisfied that "a salutary climate of peace would quickly return throughout all of Viet Nam as if a magic wand had been waved." First of all, his statement conveys the feeling that there is a formula to be found which would transform straight away the moral frame of mind among the Vietnamese. There is the implication that a modernized mandate of heaven would be found through a fairy's wand instead of through the traditional intervention of a transcendent will.

Moreover, there is an indication that this magic formula should consist of a harmonious accord with the presently prevailing world order. Historic Viet Nam would really get its bearings, Tran Van Huu was saying, if it were a member of the United Nations. Under such an international constellation Viet Nam would again feel integrated into a protective cosmos, into a world united "under heaven," *Thiên hà*. The words "way," *tạo*, and "reason," *ly*, would recover their traditional dimension—that of a coherent world in which Viet Nam's place was widely recognized.

Traditionally, Vietnamese popular opinion is apt to give great weight to the argument of international recognition of its status and may in some instances consider it decisive. However, any such ideal as internationalism carries weight with the masses only if it offers unity and security in their rural world: the equivalent of a Chinese Peace. There is, of course, little point to recalling how many times in earlier centuries this Chinese hegemony over Viet Nam has been powerless to assure internal order. Indeed, the Vietnamese conviction is that the unification of the world into some system of order is also subject to eclipse, with everything falling into disorder—this is precisely what they see in the world today. The choice they now face is not a peaceful pursuit of their national destiny but a demand that Vietnamese take sides with one of the two factions in the cosmic division of the world. They are being asked to defend their unity as a nation by fighting against large numbers of their countrymen who allied with the other side in the cosmic world order!

The Western mind sees unity as a goal that must be achieved whatever the ways and means. But nothing is more contrary to such an approach for achieving unity than the Vietnamese wait-and-see policy—except an allusion to the wave of a magic wand as the only means of overcoming it. There is a dynamism among the Vietnamese, however, which is perhaps equal to ours in the West, although it is oriented differently. It is found in the crucial word *háa*, meaning "to civilize, to change, to transform." As a matter of fact, the word appears in most plans for modernization of Vietnamese society, where it is used to emphasize the necessity of first transforming *oneself* in harmony with the demands and possibilities of the century. A whole civilization is expressed in that feeling. According to what is most alive in Vietnamese traditions, if one takes on the character and virtue of existing circumstances one may feel assured that fate and men will perceive the object of their waiting and will come to a decision about human order. The political solution that conveys this adherence will be obtained before any impression is given of its having been worked on.

For Vietnamese popular opinion there are two criteria in politics: heaven and man. Heaven has not yet come to a decision in Vietnam. As for man, what is there to say? One of the first points established in this study was the powerful and singular interest—divinatory more than moral—in any obvious signs of integrity and selflessness during periods of crisis. The French had everything to lose by overlooking the fact that the signs given by their conduct of war and politics worked against them. This is not to say that their client, the Bao Dai government, didn't recruit upright men as well as many who died courageously alongside French soldiers: to deny this would be to insult them as men. But one has only to turn to the rightist press or to foreign observers who were in favor of the French action in Indochina because of their anti-Communist views to realize what an unfortunate effect the spectacle of the war had on the Vietnamese. What matters most then and now is the people's reaction.

Paul Mus cites a personal experience in which the Vietnamese wait-and-see policy takes on a meaning that is hard to disregard. "I can still see the modest house where in 1947 I met one of my Vietnamese friends—the equal in our language to one of our best writers—who was living there in voluntary retirement because he strongly objected to any association with the Communists. Yet he also found it impossible to go along with what we French were offering. The family, which formerly had been well-to-do, was supported by the young women who courageously earned the family's living by becoming the equivalent of our fruit and vegetable peddlers. Is this enough of an answer to the predictable objection: If they're not waiting for us what are they waiting for, Communism?"

Historically, this Vietnamese reaction is neither opportunism nor a secret choice; it is a test. What the Vietnamese seek in heaven and in man are facility and austerity: facility proclaims the decision and austerity prepares for it. The Vietnamese were alarmed at the signs they saw concerning French chances in the First Indochina War; they did not believe France could prevail, so they adopted a wait-and-see attitude. Did the French ever really grasp this wait-and-see spirit, which is so similar to their own way of thinking in certain areas of behavior but is so different from that of the Vietnamese?

Vietnamese opinion in the French occupied zone made three observations concerning the objective background of the situation during the war: they were for France, against France, or in between. The most resolute Vietnamese partisans of the French were those who ignored the dangers inherent in the dishonesty of the French conduct of the war; the significance of this observation is formidable. Secondly, in the French zone there were men and families who lived in a state of abstention and retirement, and who were the prey of suspicion or police action, sometimes at great cost; they were following a classical attitude of passive disapproval and they put themselves through this test as well as anyone who opposed their refusal. Theirs was an almost ritual attitude; an extreme form of it is the creditor who remains at the door of the debtor without eating.

Strange movements and reactions, but such are the kind one encounters when one tries to set up a certain kind of politics so far from home. When the French denounced the wait-and-see policy as dangerous, they did not consider its adherents as equally neutral as regards the adversary and themselves; France considered those who abstained as her enemies. For example, recall the striking words of General de Lattre, the French commander-in-chief in Indochina in 1951, "Join the Viet Minh and you will find men who are fighting well for a bad cause!" If as a criterion we take austerity—often identified as integrity—the three attitudes shown by those who are for, against, and between seem unfavorable to France from a local point of view. Yet even if they are unfair, it is those attitudes that are decisive.

True, the French denounced the Communistic tendencies of their adversaries as morally pernicious; they recalled the deadly effect these principles would have on the moral and sociological structure of Viet Nam. But let us not forget that they were speaking to a people whom the Chinese influence has made skeptical of any declarations made by a power that doesn't have total command of a situation. Everything the French said in the hope that the Vietnamese would become involved in the war appeared to them above all as being their own business. After all, who doesn't denounce his enemies? France began by declaring that the Viet Minh were no more than a "handful of escaped convicts," but likening political convicts to common-law convicts has rarely been a rewarding argument, especially when racial opposition is involved.

In Viet Nam saying such things about one's adversaries simply means that one doesn't get along with them, so it was natural that subsequent French denunciations of Communism and its dangers were heard with the same skepticism. For the Vietnamese people the opposition in the Viet Minh ranks stood for no more than a program of moderate socialization. The people then told themselves, If the Communists are as dangerous as the French make them out to be and if heaven doesn't declare in France's favor and against her adversaries, it must be because her adversaries are right in maintaining that they are not Communists. The weak ingenuity of French propaganda stumbled here.

Anti-Communism Is Not a Formula for the Modernization of Viet Nam

Upon Paul Mus's return to Saigon in 1945, with the French commander-in-chief, General Leclerc, he met with the local French group of Marxists and asked them what the French Communists in Indochina felt about the Vietnamese Communists. "There are no French or Vietnamese Communists," we were answered. "There is one Communist Party and here we're in Indochina." Here was a parallel of the fact that in earlier years Ho Chi Minh when living in France could just as well represent the French Communist Party outside of France as a Frenchman could. But besides these bonds of common identity the party's strength is enhanced by its assertion that "purging" the capitalist, militarist, and colonialist superstructures the Communist system assures the occupants of a given territory the chance for "national" self-determination. We in the West must realize this formula to have a very convincing appeal in a world fashioned by the Chinese idea that international peace must result not from the domination of a country or an empire as such but from the sovereign expansion throughout the world of a way of life and thought.

France should have approached the Vietnamese with an eye not to her own fears and uncertainties but to theirs. The arguments of anti-Communism which the French put forward no longer had much appeal for the Vietnamese in the 1950's even though they had been attracted to them at the outbreak of the conflict. The French felt that the priority they were giving to anti-Communism would make the Vietnamese accept the human imperfections of French activities. Yet, in order to justify themselves in contrast to Communism, they would have had to give signs of the ease of their achievements as well as an austere and exemplary rigor in their political, administrative, and personal behavior. The "mystique" that the French wanted to propose to Viet Nam could not, however, be fulfilled when the non-Communist Vietnamese were so largely uncommitted to broader identities.

For them to have been integrated into an intelligible world order an establishment "under heaven" of a single unified program of politics would have been required. During the whole period of colonial rule there was a hiatus in the moral order of the Vietnamese which took the form of apparent acceptance of French control. Such an acceptance may be explained by the Vietnamese expectation that a new moral order would appear once the French interregnum had run its course. The masses were taught to believe that this moral order would spring forth through a decree of fate, and here is where Tran Van Huu's magic wand would be needed. Up until the 1920's at least, the Vietnamese thought that the French had a secret and were keeping it from them.

As a result of two world wars the West has shifted its ground. In the process, East Asia became convinced that the Western world has not yet found the formula required for giving the modern era its justification and direction. What do the present circumstances tell us? First, the Communist countries form a continental Eurasian mass that is adjacent to and now merges with the old imperial Chinese world. The land routes of communication across this Eurasian land mass have always been familiar to merchants and to revolutionaries, but they have not been the routes that brought the civilization of the Western world. Instead we of the West have come by way of the sea, which has given East Asians the impression that we have originated in island civilizations which they feel are subordinate in status. "Never trust a man who was born on an island," an old Vietnamese once told me. The prejudice is not only political but moral. Islands are a dispersion of man and God: we therefore do not have one sole religion.

What we have learned about Vietnamese sociology will at least spare us the illusion that very religious peoples prefer several religions to none at all. What they seek and call religion is, with certain exceptions, not Christian grace in all its conflicting forms or any other spiritual revelation; it is an intelligible principle that can impose one sole discipline on the world. The rigor with which Marxism means to master all sciences, institutions, and man's works as a whole may therefore be taken from the Asian perspective as the traditional sign of a call to power and political order. In this respect, the Confucian state can be seen as a precedent: its place has never been taken by a European successor because of the Western world's inability up until now to unite and to unify, or even to see society as a whole.

The profound differences between the ways of Marxism and those of the Chinese tradition, though irreconcilable, are seen as the justification of a new age. In China the evolution of a revolutionary doctrine has been an attempt to adopt a belief to the requirements of becoming the substitute of a Confucian state. With this heritage of a divine calling, it would seem natural in Eastern Asia for Marxism to assume the classical task of the Middle Kingdom—that of constituting a world order in itself. Here is a perspective of the greatest significance for the future of Viet Nam. Will its reconstruction and modernization be carried out in cooperation with the Western democracies or in a Marxist Asia?

Epilogue:

The Meaning of Revolution in Viet Nam

Is there a meaning to revolution in Viet Nam? Do the seemingly kaleidoscopic events of the past quarter of a century add up to something more than a situation of apparent anarchy? Can a pattern really be discerned in the struggle for power that has devastated Vietnamese society for more than a generation? Yes, there is a pattern, these events do have a larger significance, and there is an easily understood meaning to revolution in Viet Nam. This meaning is best explained by first referring to the contrasting bases of power between the two principal competitors in the struggle and then pointing out how these differing sources of strength have affected the pattern of conflict that has now persisted into the 1970's.

The revolutionary struggle in Viet Nam is a conflict between two modern cultures created by antagonists who still share an old culture in common. Both sides in the struggle want the same thing: a new Viet Nam that is united, independent of foreign involvement, and modern in its economy and society. The differences between them over how to achieve this new Viet Nam are not, however, merely political in the sense of being a disagreement over short-run strategies and priorities. These differences are much more profound. They are cultural, which is to say that they are based on sharply contrasting conceptions of the way a modern society ought to be organized. They clash over opposing ideas about social status and social cohesion, over what a man's place in society should be and what values should link him to other men.

Too frequently, the values of a society have been regarded by

Westerners, especially Americans, as the same thing as ethics and morality. Values and morality are, of course, inseparably interwined. But values are more than principles for personal conduct; they are also sources of social cohesion and guides for social action. Without common values men find it difficult to work together toward common goals. They either don't trust each other or they don't understand each other. Words don't have the same meaning to people who have different values. Moreover, without the discipline derived from shared values the efforts of men lack force and can easily be dissipated by quarrelsome divisions among them. In a society like the one in Viet Nam, where old values are no longer relevant to the new lives men must live, conflict over values is not merely an ethical and moral controversy—it is also, and most conspicuously, a struggle over political power.

It is because they are so critical in determining the capacity of people to work together that questions of values are also questions of power. In the most general sense, power is the ability to affect people's actions or, simply, the ability to get compliance with a demand. In politics, power implies sanctions for noncompliance, and these sanctions often depend on coercion and force. But power based solely on coercion is an extreme that is normally avoided, because it is more difficult to maintain and less dependable than power based on common values. When values are shared, people usually comply readily with demands made upon them, because they accept the legitimacy of these demands. This is why those whose power is primarily coercive always seem to try to get their values accepted by the people they wish to control. Voluntary compliance, their actions seem to confirm, will be a more certain and less arduous way of holding power within a society than coercion.

From the perspective of the role of cultural values in Vietnamese politics, the powerlessness over the past qurater-century of pro-Western, urban-oriented governments becomes easier to understand. These governments have, by and large, been limited to urban bases of power precisely because they have not had values relevant to the lives which village people have had to lead.

The sharp dichotomy in culture between the cities, where about one-fourth of the Vietnamese live, and the countryside, where about three-fourths live, has been a barrier which these governments have not really been able to overcome.

They have, of course, tried to exercise authority in the rural areas, but primarily through administrative representatives and military force. These instruments, strong though they have been at times, have not been transformed into durable power because rural people have not respected them as legitimate institutions of authority or complied with their decisions. Even if there were no rural-based revolutionaries, these governments, it seems, would still have had difficulty in conducting such routine functions as collecting taxes and administering public programs.

Generalizations about the numerous pro-Western governments that have come and gone over the past twenty-five years are, admittedly risky. These governments have run the political gamut from a transparently colonial regime under the ex-emperor Bao Dai, to a self righteous dictatorship under Ngo Dinh Diem, to the rule of American-trained military officers under Nguyen Van Thieu. But despite their differences in style these governments have had a conspicuous common denominator: a dependence on foreign troops and foreign financing to keep them in existence.

This dependence can be brought into clearer focus by recounting the steady expansion of pro-Western military forces in Viet Nam during the past several decades. As late as 1938, seven years before revolution broke out, only 11,000 French troops aided by a 16,000 man Vietnamese militia were able to maintain France's colonial control throughout the whole of Indochina—an area nearly half again as large as France itself. But after the revolution was launched a force that dwarfed this colonial contingent of the thirties was able to control very little territory on any permanent basis. Up until 1954, an expeditionary force of 70,000 French regulars, 68,000 Legionnaires and Africans, and 300,000 Vietnamese—or a total of about 450,000 men—fought in vain to uphold the claim of Bao Dai's regime, the State of Viet Nam, to be the only government for the whole country from the China border in the north to the Gulf of Thailand in the south. Though these forces were potent enough to capture territory they could not get the compliance from rural people that less than 30,000 troops had gotten in 1938.

As the 1970's begin, military forces in Viet Nam have grown to a size dwarfing even those that existed in the early 1950's. Yet the political future of the Saigon government, which has tried to rule in only the southern portion of Viet Nam, remains in doubt. Its military support, however, consists of over a million men—more than twice as great as the force which fought to sustain the Bao Dai regime. Why has there been this greater and greater dependency on foreign forces in a vain attempt to hold on to a smaller and smaller amount of territory? Why is it that 538,000 Americans plus their air and naval firepower cannot quell the armed opposition to the Siagon government? What has happened in Viet Nam to make it impossible for truly massive Western military force to prevail in Viet Nam in the 1970's when only 11,000 French troops were able to control a vastly larger territory with hardly firing a shot just thirty years before?

Some American critics feel that Western military power in Viet Nam has been unduly shackled by political constraints. Without restrictions on heavy bombing and orders against "hot pursuit" of the enemy into privileged sanctuaries, the military results of the war, they believe, would have been quite different. In the French era of the fighting they would have advocated the massive bombing of Dien Bien Phu by American air power and the denial of a safe haven across the China border to the Viet Minh. In the American era they have called for the bombing of Haiphong and the end of sanctuaries in Cambodia, Laos, and northern Viet Nam itself. These criticisms and others like them are calculations about power, specifically about the military power balances in the war, and it is natural that they should be made. But these calculations don't go far enough. They don't explain the enormous change between 1938 and 1970 in the effects of military power and the quantity of it required to have an impact in Viet Nam. They don't get at the very essence of the power relationships in the struggle in Viet Nam.

The reason these criticisms have been able to explain so little about the military dilemmas in Viet Nam is not hard to understand. Expectations about the war—by both critics and supporters alike—have been based on the usually correct assumption that most armies are trained to fight for control over territory. Armies must have bases, sources of supply, avenues of retreat, and rear-area sanctuaries where they can regroup. All the requirements for keeping an army in the field clearly point to the need for a territorial base. And since adversaries normally expect each other to defend the territorial sources of their strength, they measure the prospects for victory by their capacity to capture the other's territory.

More important than these tactical considerations, armies must control territory because they are instruments of governments which are committed to protect the people they govern. Governments are usually thought to derive their legitimacy through the exercise of sovereign authority over a territory, and when they can no longer control such a territory their legitimacy is brought into question. But in Viet Nam, Communist-led revolutionaries have won widespread political legitimacy and secured military bases without having to rely on territorial sovereignty.

The Communist substitute for territorial control has been a political link tying together a steadily larger portion of the people in the countryside. So resilient has this tie been that it does not depend on military protection to be maintained. So formidable is the power derived from this popular link that it is hard to overestimate it. In military terms alone it has meant that the Communists have almost never had to defend territory or fixed positions. Since their adversaries, the pro-Western governments, have, by contrast, depended almost entirely on control over territory as their primary source of legitimacy, an asymmetrical pattern of warfare has developed. In fighting each other the two contenders have been pursuing quite different strategic goals—goals which are obvious indications of the sharply contrasting bases of power the antagonists have depended upon.

Although the scale of the war has escalated enormously during the quarter-century since revolution broke out, the asymmetry of the conflict has remained substantially the same. The Communists' goal in mobilizing the potential power of the rural people by organizing them politically has been to tie down larger and larger numbers of their opponent's troops in static defense of territory. This strategy has struck at the critical vulnerability in pro-Western governments: their dependence on military force to maintain political power. If they abandoned their static positions they would lose control over a segment of the rural population and possibly not be able to win it back again. Yet by remaining in static positions they become convenient targets for their elusive enemy and they also lack the mobility to seize the initiative to search out and pursue the quick-moving Communist units. Here is how the quagmire has been made, here is why more and more troops have been required: to maintain political power by occupation of territory. Here is why Viet Nam has been a war not for land but for people.

The disadvantages to pro-Western governments from such a strategy are so clear that their continuing need for extra military power should not be surprising. Without a means of transforming control over territory into popular political loyalties, these governments have simply not been able to compete on the same plane with their Communist adversaries. They have had no choice but to rely on military force; it has been virtually the only instrument of power they have possessed. Its effectiveness, however, has declined, and the amount of it required to hold on to portions of the countryside has mounted as the Communists' village-based political organization has grown. Unlike 1938 or 1945 or even 1960, popular compliance caused by coercive sanctions is in deep decline; coercive power now finds itself thwarted by the power developed around a set of common values that have slowly been adopted by ever-larger segments of village Viet Nam.

This book has tried to analyze in cultural terms how and why the Communists have been successful in mobilizing political power in Viet Nam. Among the many reasons for Communist success the most essential one is the relevancy of their values to the lives villagers must lead. This relevancy springs from a conception of society as a communal as distinct from a secular organization—a conception which offers a comprehensive explanation for a new sense of community in which rural people can participate.

The longing for a new sense of community has been no abstraction among village people. Their spiritual traditions have left them with the belief that men must be linked closely together in a bond of communal identity. But as a practical matter this spirituality has not offered values explicit enough to make this bond a reality. The need has been for values to replace the Confucian traditions which once linked the villagers to a larger community and gave them a sense of being able to acquire a status of recognized significance. The relevance of Communist values, therefore, has been in the possibility of using them to establish a new communal spirit guided by the traditions and forms of the past.

Relevant though they are, these values have not been adopted in the Vietnamese countryside without great violence and extreme coercion. The struggle over who is to govern in the villages of Viet Nam and how, has, certainly, been one of the most tragic examples of political violence since the end of World War II. Moreover, even if the Communist-led revolution had not been opposed by the French, the Americans, and the anti-Communist Vietnamese, there still would have been violence—the rural people are unlikely to have accepted a new scheme of values through a peaceful mass conversion.

Rarely have the values by which people live been changed fundamentally without a fight. Even in their vestigial form the values which tenuously held Vietnamese villages together prior to 1945 conferred status on some villagers and denied it to others. A change in values meant, therefore, a loss of status to the privileged, and from the first days of the revolution village notables have, almost routinely, lost their lives. But a change in values has also meant an opportunity for an increase in status for villagers who otherwise would have led dreary lives of little consequence within a static village hierarchy.

Worse than the dreariness was the uncertainty—the lack of any really precise identity within a declining village community that also had lost its own identity. How did one establish his distinctiveness under such circumstances? There no longer were examinations in Confucian learning to set a standard for achievement. Also unlike earlier eras, there was no new land to be opened up in the south to which one could move from one's home village. There was only the limited horizon of the village—a village no more a part of a spiritually endowed kingdom but now the object of alien bureaucratic control. Then came the revolution. Along with the new ideas came a way to act upon them. There were a multitude of new organizations to be formed, all of them having a legitimacy as part of the revolution and conveying a new status for those who participated in their activities.

Although access to this new form of status has been open to everyone in the countryside—even landowners if they agreed to a redistribution of their lands—advancement to higher status positions of authority has been strictly based on performance. In much the same way that examinations testing a person's knowledge of Confucian traditions once determined who would be chosen as mandarins, a knowledge of the ideology of revolution has become the criterion for choosing the new, revolutionary cadre from the village people of Viet Nam. Written examinations, of course, are now archaic; the real test of a person's knowledge of the revolutionary program comes in action. If he is to be successful the beginning revolutionary will need not merely a spirit of daring but also a capacity to mobilize his fellow villagers and coordinate their actions within the larger scheme of revolutionary strategy.

Mastery of the ideas and values of revolution has, therefore, become a source of power and an opportunity for upward mobility in the Vietnamese countryside. By contrast with Confucian learning, this mastery has not required years of enforced inactivity for studying the Chinese language in order to learn the classics of Confucius in their original version. Mastery has come through action—action that teaches the need for acceptance of new values as a means of establishing discipline and motivation in even the smallest village guerrilla team. In other words, mastery over these values has come through using them and recognizing that the greater their acceptance the more successful the revolution—and the larger the opportunity for upward mobility.

This access to political power by Vietnamese villagers is the most essential characteristic in the meaning of revolution in Viet Nam. It represents a new way of mobilizing and sharing power that is not only a unique departure from the country's past experience in organizing political power but is also a prime example of the worldwide phenomena of the entry of peasant people into modern "mass" politics. Through revolution instead of economic development and industrialization these villagers have had their first chance to abandon passive lives of unchanging routine and by action of their own initiative to acquire a totally new status. Officer rank in the army and leading cadreman in the revolutionary party have been the most sought after positions. But because of the enormous number of local organizations for mobilizing the countryside in tying down enemy troops and supporting revolutionary forces, there have been plenty of opportunities for participation.

The popular responsiveness to these opportunities for participation has resulted in a revolutionary movement powerful enough to dominate northern Viet Nam and to stalemate a massive American force in the south for over five years. A major explanation of the motivation for this response is the relevancy of revolutionary values to Vietnamese traditions. But probably as important has been the feeling that within the revolutionary movement there is a predictability and equity in the access to power. At the lowest levels there seems to be a tested conviction that mobility to positions of authority comes to those whose performance is most notable. And throughout the movement a firm belief appears to exist in a kind of simple justice: the sharing of power on the basis of a mastery of the values and strategy of revolution.

Yet if there is a relevancy of the values of the revolution to Vietnamese traditions and if there is a sense of equity in the sharing of power within the movement, then why hasn't the revolutionary cause been adopted by all Vietnamese? Why has the revolutionary struggle gone on for so long? Why does a substantial portion of Vietnamese society still oppose the revolution? All revolutions have, naturally, been opposed by those who benefit from an existing regime as well as those who are uncertain about what a future regime might bring. But as protracted as revolutions usually are, few have endured as long as has revolution in Viet Nam. Foreign intervention has, of course, made a major difference by prolonging and intensifying the conflict through the commitment of troops to fight on behalf of pro-Western governments.

From this intensity have come deeper cleavages in Vietnamese society and an emphasis by both sides in the struggle on coercion in winning political allegiance. Terror and brutality have mounted as techniques for obtaining popular bases of power as the war has escalated. It is impossible and undoubtedly useless to attempt to assess which side has been the most brutal. Neither side has clean hands. Their conflict has made pawns out of fellow Vietnamese; the score is now kept by the number of their countrymen each side can claim to "control." But despite the inhumaneness of this violence an assessment can be made about its consequences and, particularly, about its relevance to the meaning of revolution in Viet Nam.

The Communist revolutionaries have prided themselves on the selective use of terror. By carefully relating their terror tactics to specific political goals, they have sought to break down the resistance of vestigial village cohesion and to persuade the villagers to adopt their scheme of revolutionary values. Killing a rich landowner or an informer for the pro-Western governments has been their way of communicating both revolutionary goals and revolutionary power. Forcing young villagers to join local militia units and then indoctrinating them on the strategy of revolution has been their technique of winning new recruits by force. When terror is indiscriminate, they feel, people may be drawn together out of a common fear rather than being divided and won over through tactics which forcefully yet skillfully coerce them to become a part of the revolutionary movement.

Pro-Western governments in Viet Nam have never relied on tactics of selective terror. Their political goals have instead called for force to be used in occupying and controlling territory. Somehow they have expected this control to lead to political allegiance. Perhaps they have thought that if rural people were given some protection they would be grateful. Yet, clearly, they have expected too much from such a concept of passive allegiance. But a more active form of popular allegiance has been out of the question. Pro-Western governments have simply been unwilling to share power with the people in the countryside. In part this has been motivated by a desire to have power concentrated in a few hands.

Yet beyond such selfishness there has been the larger problem of being unable to devise a scheme of values to form the base of a community encompassing the modern world of the cities and the traditional world of the villages. Without any values to master as a means of gaining access to power and without local-level organizations for participation in national politics, allegiance from the countryside has been lacking.

In the discussion of the alienation of the Westernized elite from Vietnamese traditions, this book tried to suggest some of the reasons why Viet Nam's upper class has not been able to offer leadership to the countryside. Divorced from their country's past, these new mandarins have nevertheless expected and demanded the compliance that previous Vietnamese elites had gotten. Yet they have not realized that this earlier compliance was based on shared values. The old mandarins were respected because their intellectual achievement could be measured in terms that villagers understood and according to values by which villagers lived. These country people cannot now share the values on which this new Westernized upper class is founded because for them they are unattainable. These values were obtained primarily through education in an alien scientific culture. If, earlier, this upper class had tried to relate their modern values to the world of the village, they might have won the loyalty of the villagers for which they have been fighting. But they have been an exclusivist upper class, concerned more with the maintenance of their privileges than in forming a community with the countryside.

Increasingly larger military forces have been required to maintain anti-Communist, urban-oriented governments in Viet Nam. The political impact of these forces has, however, been disproportionately small in comparison with their massive size. The governments they have desperately tried to sustain have steadily been losing ground because they have been unable to consolidate the potential power which military force has given them in the Vietnamese countryside. Clearly the meaning of this tragic conflict is that force alone cannot cope with the mass mobilization of peasant people for involvement in revolutionary struggle. Without some competitive program for mobilizing and sharing power in the countryside Western military force can only fight a rear-guard action.

This book has tried to bring a fresh perspective to the repetitious pattern of conflict in Viet Nam by emphasizing some time-tested insights about the nature of Vietnamese society. Despite the enormous scale of violence and the far-reaching changes in the country the most important aspects of the struggle remain the same. Pro-Western governments are still trying to wrest control over the countryside away from rural-based revolutionaries who have developed power by relating their strategy and values to Vietnamese traditions. The meaning of revolution in Viet Nam is that the opportunity for predictable access to political power by village people is a more potent form of power than a primarily military force arrayed against them. In Viet Nam, therefore, the technological power of the West has had its weaknesses exposed by the political power of a peasant people. The embarrassment this exposure has brought might well have been avoided, of course, if, sometime over the twenty years since the ideas in this book were first presented, the meaning of revolution in Viet Nam had been understood.

BIBLIOGRAPHY
Major Published Works of Paul Mus

Barabudur: esquisse d'une histoire du Bouddhisme fondée sur la critique archéologique des textes. Hanoi, 1935.

La Mythologie primitive et la pensée de l'Inde. Paris, 1937.

La Lumière sur les six voies: Tableau de la transmigration bouddhique. Paris, 1938.

Le Viet-Nam chez lui. Paris, 1946.

Viet-Nam: sociologie d'une guerre. Paris, 1952.

Le Destin de l'Union Française de l'Indochine à l'Afrique. Paris, 1954.

Guerre sans visage, lettres commentées du Sous-Lieutenant Émile Mus. Paris, 1961.

INDEX

DATE DUE